Jam Butties
and a
Pan of Scouse

Jam Butties and a Pan of Scouse

Hardship and happiness in the Liverpool docks

MAGGIE CLARKE

AND

CATHRYN KEMP

TRAPEZE

This edition first published in Great Britain in 2016 by
Trapeze
an imprint of the Orion Publishing Group Ltd
Carmelite House
50 Victoria Embankment
London EC4Y 0DZ
An Hachette UK Company

1 3 5 7 9 10 8 6 4 2

A CIP catalogue record for this book
is available from the British Library.

ISBN: 978 1 4091 6676 4

Typeset by Input Data Services Ltd, Bridgwater, Somerset

Printed and bound by CPI Group (UK) Ltd, Croydon, CR0 4YY

www.orionbooks.co.uk

Contents

CHAPTER I

Abandoned

26–27 June 1931

Our hobnail boots clattered on the cobbled road as we ran, shrieking with laughter. Me, my brother Tommy and our sister Nellie hopped and skipped our way up Latimer Street, shouting our glee so that everyone in the surrounding streets could hear us.

'Did ye see the food, like? There was piles of it!' giggled Tommy, brushing his dark hair out of his face, which was alive with excitement.

Tommy was a small, stocky boy of eight years old. He was the spitting image of our father Thomas Riley. Nellie, whose real name Ellen we never used, and at three years old was the baby of the family, had our mam's softer looks, with her fair hair and piercing blue eyes. Me? I looked like my da; even at the tender age of ten I could see my resemblance to the gentle, loving man who still kissed us on the foreheads each night as he came in from a day's work. I had his nose, his dark hair, but I had also inherited my mam Mary's eyes, the colour of cornflowers, or so I was told.

Just then I stopped running. I bent over to catch my breath, exclaiming: 'And the cakes, they had proper buns with sugar on!' I turned round to see my breathless siblings, their huge smiles lighting up their small faces.

'I'm goin' to be sick, our Maggie!' exclaimed toddler Nellie, grinning her babyish smile, as she clutched at her tummy with a playful gesture, wrinkling her smock that was smeared with jam.

'Goin' to be sick, sick, SICK!' hooted Tommy, rolling on the ground in mock agony, his knees protruding from under his long shorts and his boots kicking on the cobbles. His face was as grubby as Nellie's dress, covered in sugar from the sticky buns he had wolfed down earlier.

'Think what me mam'll say when she hears about today, she'll not believe us when we tell her about the food. The sandwiches all sliced up nice and small, like, the lemon tarts . . .' I added, closing my eyes to savour the memory of all that delicious grub. It was like heaven!

For a moment we all stopped, caught by recollections of our day out, our day of forgetting that we were the poorest of Liverpool's hardworking classes, our day of forgetting the grinding poverty of our daily lives and the deprivations we encountered. Every summer Lee Jones, or Herbert Lee Jackson Jones as he was properly known, organised a picnic for the families of the casual dock labourers that lived around our dirty streets. He was a rich man with a big heart, and his charity, the League of Welldoers, provided some of the happiest days of our childhoods, and some of the grandest feasts, even though to others it must have been simple fare.

We often didn't see a meal as regularly as we should have done, even though my father worked as many hours as he could as a docker and my mother hawked fruit, vegetables and salt from her handcart. Most of us kids didn't have winter clothes to speak of, or boots that fitted us properly, as everything we owned was hand-me-downs, many times over. We were the children whose fathers queued on the stand at the dock pen at daybreak each morning, in the hope of a day's backbreaking work unloading the cargo ships. Children like us: the poorest, most deprived and most deserving of a little kindness, perhaps, in our beloved city Liverpool.

Not that we knew much about the rest of the metropolis that stood beyond our watery dockland home. I'd only ever been as far as the gas works, and the streets that backed onto the teeming docks. Liverpool the city was as foreign to me as Iceland, but I loved it with a passion. Each summer we squealed with delight when the nuns at school announced which day we'd be off on our trip. This year it was a picnic near the League itself on Limekiln Lane, a fifteen-minute dash from our flat in number three court, number five house, Athol Street.

Athol Street was in the north end of Liverpool, running between Scotland Road and Great Howard Street. It was dissected by the Leeds/Liverpool Canal, set against the rumble of the overhead railway in the distance and the sounds from the great ships as they docked. It was a place crammed with people scratching out their existence. Disease was commonplace, vermin outnumbered the residents – just – and misfortune and poverty stalked the overcrowded tenements. And yet, it was home. We didn't know any better. We got on with our lives as best we could, swarming like river rats up and down the cobbled streets, dodging the filth and the squalor as we invented imaginary worlds.

Our neighbours were our friends, our support and even our enemies at times, but we couldn't escape each other. Our ablutions at the water pumps in the courts or the shared lavvies were public business, our days lived in each other's gaze amid the gossiping housewives, the labourers puffing on woodbines at street corners, the shrieks and calls of the street hawkers as they plied their trade, and the children commanding the streets in mock battle. Everywhere you looked there were people living close to the industrial stench and noise of the great docks that gave our city its name, and its wealth. Not that we saw any wealth, except when the great and the good like our beloved Lee Jones looked down on us and smiled. Days like today. When, for once, we were carefree and sated with more food than we'd normally see for days.

From the minute we'd been told about our picnic, we'd counted down the days, guessing what we'd eat and arguing over who would devour the most cake. The event was a highlight for us in a difficult world. We loved our home, our streets and our neighbours, but by God times were tough. By God we knew our fathers and mothers had to work long, hard hours for the few shillings they brought home each week. The Great Depression had hit our port, sweeping like wild fire across the Atlantic, or so Da had said. Poverty was nothing new to our community, but suddenly it leeched into every home, every family, it's black tendrils leaving a trail of desperation and squalor. Da would read from the newspaper, if he'd chanced upon a discarded one at the dockside, and so we knew our city had double the unemployment of the rest of the country. Well, we could've guessed that. We knew that we had to pay too much for too little to live in slum housing and pump water in the court each day of our small lives. And yet, despite the hunger, the dirt, the disease, we felt as free as birds as we careered around the cobbled roads. We were the lucky ones, we had shoes on our feet and a roof over our heads, however mean.

I blinked my eyes open. 'Come on our Tommy, our Nellie, we need to get a move on to help our mam with the pot.'

With that, we hurried our pace, chattering and whooping with the laughter of the innocent children we were. It was nearly 4 p.m. and if we didn't get a move on we'd see the back of our mother's hand for our troubles. She was always ready with her hands, a slap here, a cuff there, her arms scarred with tattoos. Always raising her voice at us kids, bustling round getting her chores done, or worse, lying in bed motionless, refusing to speak to us while her black moods were on her. Even Da couldn't rouse her from those internal tempests, and that was saying something because she could usually find something to moan or yell at him about. Her tempers were the backdrop to our family life, which is why we loved our escapes out of the tiny rooms so much. I knew she drank. Tommy and Nellie were too young to understand properly, but I'd seen the bottles of grog discarded under the iron bedframe we all shared. I'd smelt her sour breath after a day spent falling in and out of the pubs on Scottie Road. And if I hadn't noticed those things then I'd have soon found out from the gossip by our well-meaning neighbours.

I'd surely have known from that, and the fact that the little furniture and possessions we had ended up, often as not, inside the pawnbrokers for the price of a day's ale. Da would bring home orange boxes pilfered from the dockyards so we'd have something to sit on to eat our dinner, telling the younger ones it was a game. But I knew. I knew it wasn't normal to sit on orange boxes while Mam spent the pennies she'd raised on booze. When she'd finished that money, she'd sing at the pub's piano for a few more scoops of ale. She had a beautiful voice, but a rotten soul, so help me God for saying it.

Chatter was all most of the women did round here each day, in between scrubbing the steps of the tennies (our word for tenements), washing nappies while breastfeeding their multiples of children, and getting their old man's dinner on the range before he came home hungry, or drunk, or both. Gossip was the fabric of our community, the coping mechanism for all our hurts and indignities. For sure, there was nothing private here in Athol Street, and there was nothing those women didn't know about my mother's problem with the beer. Many times I watched as Mam staggered between the range and the small wooden table in the larger of the two rooms we shared, swearing and cursing for all to hear.

'All right, queen?' Da would say. 'Why don't ye sit down and let me get them plates . . .?'

But she'd bat off his hand, the kindness of his gesture, and swivel round, her eyes blazing, and give him a verbal dose of whatever blackness lay inside her. Her lovely hair would always be dishevelled, her apron dirty, and even though many would call her pretty-looking, I cringed from her even as a child. I always turned away when my father tried to placate her. I could never bear to see my father being treated with such disdain. I knew that many a woman on this road would get a beating for the same behaviour, but her rejection of Da's gentle ways stung me more than a slap ever would.

By the time we turned into the narrow passageway leading to the court we called home, my stomach was turning over with nerves. *Will she be drunk again?* I fervently hoped not, more for Tommy and Nellie's sakes than for myself. I wanted to protect them from Mam's drinking for as long as I could, but it was getting harder and harder as her drunkenness became more frequent with each passing week.

I looked up, half-expecting Mother to be hanging out of the small window of our ground floor flat, a regular Molly Malone with her handcart by the door and whatever remained of her wares slung into the cooking pot, but instead saw only the black, soot-coated tenement standing four stories high. It faced another building, which was just as bleak, creating our small court where the water pump stood as the open drain sliced through the cobbles. Every winter the water froze, then every spring the tap thawed and dripped water, making muddy pools of filth that formed slick pools under our feet. Lines of washing hung in drooping surrender between the windows of each building, strung across the court in an assortment of grey knickers, pants, vests and shirts swaying gently in the slight June breeze, blocking whatever of the day's light had filtered down through the soot and the smoke. I sighed, wondering what Mam would make of us on our noisy return home, as I walked up behind Tommy and Nellie who were still wide-eyed with wonder.

'Beware the back entry diddlers!' I called to our Tommy and our Nellie as they scampered through the drooping drawers and vests. The Back Entry Diddlers were the shady characters who preyed on poor people like us, skulking in the shadows selling stolen goods and offering to lend money. Da always told us to stay clear of them as they hung around small, cramped courts like ours, flirting with the housewives and handing out occasional sweets to the children. No policemen ever came down our jigger, which was the name we gave to the back entry to the courts, so we were as vulnerable as mice hunted by cats in our cramped alleys and doorways. Luckily there were no strangers there today, just the usual neighbours laughing, swearing, crossing themselves, hanging out washing and walloping passing children as they screeched and wailed.

Inside our flat the room was dark. I could see my mam's faded apron lying over one of the upturned orange boxes, but her boots and hat were missing. *She must be out getting in food fer dinner*, I thought to myself, surprised that she wasn't home as it was getting on and Father would be back from work soon. Even if she'd spent the days in the pubs off Scottie Road, Mam was normally home, swaying like a marsh reed in the twilight or hiccupping into her hot tea. Or she'd be home, stone cold sober but mean as hell with it, and then I'd usually feel the back of her hand over some imagined misdemeanour.

Tommy had settled himself down on one of the two remaining kitchen chairs, his legs swinging off the floor. Nellie had hurtled into the bedroom that lay behind the main room, the only other in the flat apart from the scullery. It was here we all slept in the single iron bed, with its sagging stained mattress and scratchy wool blankets.

'Come 'ed, our Nellie, me mam's not in there. If she was home the range would at least be lit an' we'd have a candle goin',' I shouted to my sister, wondering where Mam was, feeling a sense of disquiet.

'Help me get somethin' on the stove will yer,' I added, because even though Nellie was little she knew to collect the wood and coke so that we could start the fire for cooking.

'Where's me mam?' Nellie asked as she walked back into our bare living room. We didn't have much. No real possessions, just a table, a tin bath that all the families in our block shared and was usually hung on a nail in the court, but which I'd lugged up the stairs for tonight's bathtime, and little else. Nothing of value. That's why we never locked our doors. There was no point. We didn't have anything to steal! Except perhaps a heel of bread, or a sack of coal, but that was it. We lived day to day and somehow we got by.

'Don't ye go worryin', our Nellie,' I said firmly. 'Me mam won't thank us if there's no fire goin' fer our dinner when she's back. She's probably out there, mithering the butcher for a scrap of meat.' I forced a laugh, suddenly feeling uneasy again. Mammy had been late before. She might even still be working on the streets, calling her wares in her lilting Irish accent.

Later, when I'd got a pot going on the stove and added neeps, potatoes and a few mouldy carrots, the door opened and there was Da. He beamed a big smile of welcome, as we rushed into his open arms.

'Have ye been good children today, eh?' he said.

He always said that when he came in. His voice was soft, partly because he was almost stone deaf by being badly hurt when he fell through a ship's hold while unloading its cargo several years earlier. The fall had ripped off his ear, damaging both his ear drums. There was no compensation for his injuries, the idea was laughable. Instead, he was docked a day's pay and sent to the hospital to get patched up. The minute he could walk again he was back on the ships, carrying vast loads of spices and timber, but unable to hear the sounds of the bustling dockyards any longer.

'Dinner's on,' I shouted up at him, breathing in his homely, familiar smell of oil, spices and sweat.

He smiled and kissed me on the forehead. 'She's not back yet?' he added, casting his eyes around the dimly lit room.

'Not yet, Da,' I replied, 'she must be makin' a fortune out there today.'

'Aye she must, our Maggie, yer a good girl.' And he turned away towards Nellie who was clutching at the fabric of his trousers with wild-eyed excitement.

'Now then, me beauty, what did ye do today?' he smiled, as if he hadn't known. Tommy and Nellie had chattered on about the Lee Jones picnic every day for the past month!

As my siblings talked, I watched the pot. I lit a candle as dusk fell over our streets. The noises from outside were tailing off as the dockers, coal heavers, ship's scalers and mill workers went home for their teas. The women and children disappeared inside the tennies at 5 p.m. for whatever dinner was due to be put on the table, and the horses and their loads of cargo and produce were taken off to wherever they'd come from. It was the only time of the day our streets were anything like peaceful.

The coke smog from the gas works seemed to settle onto our buildings and roads, lying like a dark veil, silencing the docks. My mam was still nowhere to be seen. By the time we'd finished the poor gruel I'd cobbled together, it was time to boil up the water for Tommy and Nellie's bath, a laborious process that took me most of the evening. Once everyone had had a turn in the quickly cooling water, with the bar of red carbolic soap and an old sheet for drying ourselves, it was time to settle the little ones in bed.

Father usually took us through to tell us a story while we snuggled up together, but tonight he sat staring into the embers of the range fire, quiet and still. I guessed he was waiting for Mam to come home. I did Da's job myself, and soon both Tommy and Nellie were fast asleep, Nellie with her thumb in her mouth. I watched them both, their eyelids fluttering as they dreamed their way to tomorrow, my heart so filled with love for them it was fit to burst.

Why then did I feel this thread of foreboding as I stroked Tommy's hair, this soft uncoiling of the fear that had been waiting for me since our arrival home? Nellie's face was pink, flushed from the effects of good food and party games. She looked even younger than her three short years in that moment, sated with the small pleasures the day had given her. Watching her made me swell with protectiveness, and something else, a steely core in me that said: whoever threatens us will never win because they'll have me to answer to.

They'd both asked again and again why their mam wasn't home when I put them to bed. Even though I was merely a child myself, many times before I'd had to step in and play at being 'mother' when Mam was too drunk to do it herself, so tonight was nothing new, except for one crucial fact: Mam always, always came home. Until now. I'd made myself smile, and say cheerily lie after lie. *She's at a friend's. She's decided to stay there overnight. She'll be here in the morning, slicing up the bread as usual, a frown on her face, but there, looking after us, as a Mam should do.* I hated lying to them, but what else could I do?

It was obvious to me that my da had no idea of her whereabouts. He said little all evening, but the next morning he donned his large flat cap, polished his docker's boots with the corner of a tatty sleeve, and left the house saying to me, and only me, that he was going to the police station, the hospital and the morgues to search for Mam, his wife of fifteen years. I was old enough to know the truth, or that's what he said.

That day at school was torture, waiting to find out if Mam was ill, injured or worse. Tommy and I grew more and more anguished with worry through the day, forcing me to keep up my cheerful chatter, and keep that smile on my face. I would rather have died myself than given my brother a moment's extra worry, but he wasn't daft, he knew something wasn't right.

By the time the school bell rang the end of the day, Tommy and I leapt from our seats and ran from St Sylvester's School in Silvester Street, all the way home to Athol Street. We burst into the main room to find our father sat at the table with Nellie on his knee. I guessed in that moment that one of our neighbours had looked after her all day, as there was no sign of Mam. My heart almost jumped out of my mouth when I saw the grim look on his face. It wasn't like Da not to be at work. Something was definitely wrong. *Our mother isn't dead, is she?* I recoiled, feeling bile rise up in my throat.

'Now don't look at me like that, our Maggie,' said Da,

looking up at our scared faces. 'She's not in the morgues or the ozzy, and the police haven't seen her.'

I exhaled, feeling like it was the first time I had properly breathed throughout the entire day. 'So, where is she then?' was all I said in reply.

Father threw me a look, one I was too young to understand. It was the kind of look that grown-ups gave each other, exchanged in a brief second of bitter understanding. A hard glance that spoke of something dark, something adult. Before I could open my mouth to ask him what he meant by it, he looked away.

With a swift move, which made me realise how deft he must be hauling hundredweight sacks from those ships holds without spilling the contents, or tipping himself off the small boats that ferried the cargo between the great ships and the dockside, he got to his feet. In one stride he was out of the door, his black wool overcoat slung over his shoulder, his large grey cap already in place over his brow. I watched him go, with a feeling that our small world was about to irrevocably change forever.

He was only gone an hour, but it felt like days. I sat, watching the clock hands move slowly round. I felt like my arms and legs were suddenly made of lead and I couldn't move, not even if the house had burnt down around me. Tommy and Nellie, being younger, were easily distracted, and Tommy had gone back to building himself a cart to wheel around the street out of an old crate and some pram wheels found in a nearby alley with some of his pals from the court. Nellie was whispering to her only doll, a small toy made out of rags, which was her heart's joy. *At least they are happy*, I mused.

Eventually, as the day turned to twilight, I roused myself

from my fears to light the range alone again. Somehow I instinctively knew I was going to have to get used to doing this, not just today but perhaps every day from now on. For a brief moment I turned to the small statue of Our Lady Mary that sat on the shelf in the kitchen and crossed myself. The statue was the first thing anyone saw on entering our home. Our only real treasure, she was a small plaster figurine with a painted blue veil and a smile of such sweetness it gave me hope that things could always, always be better for us if I just had enough faith. We always made the sign of the cross on entering and leaving, without thinking about it. But my gesture was more than just from habit today, I needed to feel I had some kind of divine protection. Again, it was just an instinct.

Then, as I was peeling the spuds, I heard Father's footsteps and he appeared in the doorway. I turned to face him and my peelings fell onto the floor from my hands, scattering into the dust. His face was ashen. His features crumpled in shock. He drew up his chair, sat on it, then fumbled with his cap, before getting up and pacing the kitchen floor. The three of us stood waiting for the bomb to land, for the shock waves to engulf us as well. When he finally spoke, this is what he said, and they are words I will never forget.

'Our Tommy, our Nellie, I want y'all to hear this as well. I've got some terrible news, terrible news, like.'

'What is it? Is me mam dead?' I cried, unable to keep hold of my fright any longer, knowing that by interrupting him the revelation would take precious moments longer. It was the day before my eleventh birthday, and yet I wailed like a child at the thought that I may have lost my mother, despite her many faults, her inattention and her love for the booze. 'Yer mam isn't dead, no, she's not dead, like. But she's not comin' back to us, that I do know, queen.' Father cleared his throat. He'd used the term 'queen' that denoted my changed status from child to responsible young woman.

The clock ticked. A bead of sweat tickled my back but this time I waited. How did Da know? Where had he been for the last hour?

'I've been down the alehouses on Scottie Road and I've been speaking to a few regulars, like. It seems yer mam, or Mary as we'll now call her as she's no mother to ye any more by doing this, Mary's gone and left us for another fella.

'She met him in the pub, drinking and laughing with him one minute, then running off with him the next.' The disbelief was etched onto my father's kind face. He slowly shook his head and continued, sitting down at last. 'They'd planned it, see. They'd planned to leave us, and now they have. Before Holy Jaysus himself I wouldn't have wished this on ye, but I have to say it, yer mother is never coming home. She's gone.'

CHAPTER 2

Life Without Me Mam

July 1931

'Our Margaret, yer doing it again, girl, wake up and pay attention!' The sound of the nun's voice cut through my daydreams, startling me back into reality. It was a hot July day, and the drone of the teacher's lesson, the heat and the buzz of flies as they danced against the window panes, had left me feeling sleepy. It didn't help that it was my least enjoyable lesson of the day: catechism. I loved my prayer book and our classes in reading and writing, but the sacraments and commandments, the dogma of our church, left my head reeling.

The extra workload on me after Mam left us was also weighing on my young mind, and on my body too. I was now 'mother' to our Tommy and our Nellie, and helpmeet to our father. This meant that every morning I'd be up at first light to start the range heating, gathering the coal, starting a fire and drawing out a small flame, enough to set the kettle to boil while I cut bread or made a pan of porridge for our breakfast. Then as the little 'uns were eating I'd sweep the wooden floors, pushing the grime out of our front door and into the court, which was already alight with noise and bustle as women queued for the water pump and gossiped with their neighbours.

I'd be out there myself with the kettle, filling it to the brim as water for tea and for washing, if I got the time. If not, it was a quick once over outside, splashing the cold water onto my half-asleep face and hands. Then once Father, Tommy and Nellie had eaten I'd gather their clothes, help my siblings dress and run a comb through their tangles before snatching a bite to eat and hurrying us all out of the door for school.

Woe betide us if we were late! The nuns were as strict about timekeeping, as they were about our moral standards, so I wouldn't always have time to feed myself and would go to my lessons hungry. At this thought, my stomach gave a growl, confirming that I'd skipped this morning's offering. Each morning Da patted me on the head as he left to queue at the dock pen, a bittersweet smile on his lips, his eyes full of sadness, but also pride at seeing how I was coping with our new situation. I couldn't bear to see his torment, so I would smile back as brightly as my exhaustion allowed and kiss his rough cheek, knowing it was just a small salve for his hurts.

I was 'Mam' in all but name, and yet I was still a young girl – on the brink of womanhood but still needing the comfort of my family life, with its hardships, deprivations but its joys and warmth as well. I yawned and turned to face the Sister, who was glaring at me from the front of the classroom. With a jolt, I sat upright and clutched my pencil, frantically trying to think what her question to me might have been. It was no good, I'd drifted off into my thoughts and knew I was now in for it!

Slowly the nun walked towards me, her starched wimple and black veil making a formidable sight. I gazed up at her and gulped. How could I possibly make the Sister understand that I was now pupil, mother and housewife? I stifled another yawn which the fearsome lady saw.

'Our Margaret, you will stand up and tell the class why you refuse to learn today, stand up so we can all see the girl who is too lazy to join us in our lesson.'

The room went deathly quiet, as the murmurings and whispers of the forty or so children in the class stopped as one, and waited with an expectant air. With that I slowly raised to my feet, my chair scraping the hard floor beneath me. Eighty eyes swivelled towards me and I gulped again. I blinked and surveyed the room. It was a large classroom, with a magnificent statue of Our Lady staring down on us with her cold, stone-carved eyes. Her veil a beautiful blue, her face a picture of Holy obedience. The desks, which sat four of us to a wooden bench, were arranged around the room in an L-shape. At the end of the classroom nearest the door was the blackboard – where the Sister had been standing, though she had now walked the length of the room to stand directly in front of me.

To me, the nun seemed to have grown ten feet taller. Her gaze was hidden behind spectacles that winked with the sunlight so I couldn't see her eyes. She was a slim, commanding sort of woman with starched morals along with her habit, and a tendency to use the ruler, hitting across the knuckles of anyone who transgressed during her lessons.

I opened my mouth to say something, anything that might diffuse the situation, though it felt hopeless, and at that moment there was a brief knock on the door and it swung open to reveal two of the Lay Sisters and, to my surprise, my young sister Nellie. My father must've brought her in to school to tell the nuns what happened at home. I gawped at the intrusion as the forty pairs of eyes moved now to the doorway.

'What is the meaning of this? Can we help you?' Raising herself up to her full height, the nun turned her sharp-looking face to the intrusion.

'I'm very sorry, Sister, but we have some pressing news to tell the children today, and our friend Nellie Riley here is goin' to share it with us all,' replied the younger of the two Sisters who'd entered the room. Her face was alight with a smile and she looked around the room at us as we waited, dumbstruck, for events to unfold.

I guess for the rest of the children it was as good as a play, but I had started to shake a little, wondering what on earth Nellie was doing and whether there was some new tragedy or challenge I was going to have to face. Since Mam had abandoned us, my experience of the world had changed beyond recognition. Whereas before she left, I knew I had to dodge her drunkenness and the occasional slap that was harder than it should've been, my view of the world was essentially a child's vision, with a young girl's cares and worries and a feeling of being safe at home with a father and a mother at the helm. But for the past two weeks since she'd been gone, my sense of security had shattered. Home was a different place.

No longer did I hear Da's laughter at Tommy's cheeky antics, or hear him crooning to Nellie when sleep didn't come easily. He was a changed man, an even more solitary man, who sat each night staring at the grimy, peeling walls of our tenement with barely a word passing his lips from sundown to sunrise. He'd taken to sleeping in his chair by the range, a sleep filled with mutterings, an uneasy dreaming time that left him grey with tiredness at the start of each day. His back was stooped, his gait that of a broken man, despite him being just forty-seven years of age. He still did his duty by us each morning, going out into the dawn to join the other men down at the docks to harry for a button given out by the dockland foreman which would guarantee him a day's work and a day's pay in his pocket. He still did what he had to, but the soul and the spirit of him seemed to have been ripped from him by his wife's desertion of us.

And me? I woke every day to the knowledge I had no

mother any more, no Mam to wipe away my childish tears, no one to soothe or comfort me, though she did little enough of that when she was around. The difference between her being there and her not being there, though, was like the gap between our bustling dockland home and the grey sea that stretched between us and the next big continent, America. It was unfathomable, vast. My sense of home was now a shifting entity under my feet, my comfort only a moment at the end of each day where I shed a quiet tear. And, I'll be honest, I cried for myself. I felt like a small girl in a big, grown up world, which I guess I now was. I felt scared and burdened by responsibility I wasn't sure I was able to shoulder.

So now here was Nellie, looking up at me with her big blue eyes, and I suddenly felt fear like an icy grip inside my belly.

'Why, our Maggie, yer already standing, ye must have known we were comin',' said the kindly nun in her broad Liverpool accent. She was shorter than my teacher, and rather plump. We used to joke that she ate all the sacrament bread, but now all I wanted was to melt into her arms and sob my worries into her full, comforting frame. I missed my mam, even though she drank, even though the bottle came before us, her children, on more occasions than I dared remember. I missed her, and I feared for Da. Were Tommy, Nellie and I about to face even worse? Had our da died at the docks which were dangerously packed with trawler men, horses and their loads, dock men, and the young boys who weaved in and out of the clamour? Was I about to learn that we'd become orphans? After all, Da did the dirtiest, hardest work at the ship sides, helping to winch enormous loads from the bowels of those great vessels, brought in by barges, which the dockers called 'flats'.

It would only take one moment of inattention, one missed instruction from the stevedores, one misplaced footing, to be crushed underneath the weight of those great carriers of grain and spices, timber and glue. One brief second in a jostling, catcalling world where human life was cheap and commerce overrode men like a great foot stamping ants on an anthill.

Our father Thomas had been hurt before. One time I'd been called out of class, on a day not unlike today, and told by one of the nuns that Da had been injured badly when run over by one of the railway wagons that travelled along the rail tracks of the docks day and night. His deafness and the darkness of the night meant he hadn't heard or seen it coming. Da hadn't been found by his fellow dockers until the next morning. He'd spent a whole night out in the cold and lost half of his left foot as a result. He always said that the pain he suffered was the reason his hair went white literally overnight. That was six years ago, and still I remembered feeling sick to my stomach with shock at hearing the news, so much so that I was sent home from school that day.

I didn't think I could bear hearing any more news like that, and yet here I was, feeling like I was on the brink of hearing something that could change my life forever. Suddenly the kindness of the Sister felt like an inadequate bandage for my fears.

That's it, I thought, *she must be tellin' us bad news, and Holy Jesus I don't think I'm ready to hear it.* Why was Nellie, who looked up at me shyly, standing in my classroom, looking like she wanted to be anywhere else but here? I had to know.

At last, I met the Sister's eye. Her face was beaming, though. Her brown eyes twinkled as I met her gaze and the tight clenching feeling in my stomach eased, just for a moment. I shook my head in bewilderment. The Sister turned then to Nellie, who looked up at her with her small, lovely face.

'Come on then our Nellie, get yerself up on the chair and tell us all yer news,' prompted the sister, holding Nellie's hand as she climbed onto an empty chair, and then onto one of the desks. I could hardly believe my eyes. Even my stern teacher looked intrigued, and normally we'd have had hell to pay for standing on the furniture in class! 'Go on girl,' whispered the nun to my little sister, 'tell them what ye told me . . .'

Here it was, whatever was coming was about to land. For a moment, I looked at Nellie and my heart bloomed with pride. She was wearing the green gym slip and white blouse I'd bought a few days' earlier from the pawn shop for six-pence. The outfit had been laid out on a table outside the shop and I couldn't help but buy it with the shillings our father gave me each week me for housekeeping money. I'd taken it home and washed it thoroughly with Reckitt's Blue soap. I wasn't having anyone say I couldn't manage, and that we wore dirty clothes. Nellie was proud as punch of her new outfit and wore it every day, so each evening I rinsed out the days' soot and dirt and put it to dry on the chair in front of the range. And here she was, her fair hair catching the light, standing on a desk in front of us all with her eyes downcast at her fraying socks and grubby old shoes.

With a soft baby voice, she whispered, 'Me mam's left an' our Maggie's become our new mam.'

'Speak up, our Nellie, so everyone can hear ye,' encouraged the kind Sister, reaching up to give her a gentle pat on the arm.

Nellie cleared her voice, and repeated what she'd said,

only this time she drew herself up and looked around at the class. 'Me mam left us, and so our Maggie's become our mam now. She does everythin' for us, even cooks our dinner every evenin', an' it doesn't even hurt when she combs me hair every mornin' ...' Her voice trailed off, and she blushed at hearing her own voice echo around the room.

The kindly nun added, 'And we've all noticed how clean and smart ye all are, even though ye don't have a Mam at home, so let that be a lesson to everyone in this room.' There was a moment's silence as the eighty eyes took in Nellie and her blushes, and me with my look of amazement, and then all of a sudden the room erupted as eighty hands started clapping, and forty mouths were suddenly cheering! I couldn't believe my eyes and ears. I'd never heard anything like it.

'Hurray fer our Maggie,' shouted one boy, smearing his face with snot.

'She's our girl,' shouted a girl from our court, clapping her hands excitedly.

I looked around at the cheering faces and allowed myself a smile that grew and grew with each second of the applause. I had never experienced anything like it. I grinned at Nellie, feeling a big lump in my throat. Here I was, about to be disciplined for my inattention, and suddenly I was being congratulated instead!

'Well done, our Nellie, now get yerself down and back to class with ye,' beamed the Sister. She looked back at me as she helped Nellie down and gave me a quick wink, just small enough so that my teacher wouldn't see. I laughed at that.

'Now, now, everyone hush. Quiet children! Back to work! We're all proud of our Margaret for taking on a mother's chores but we still have work to do.' The nun strode back to the board and rapped it with her cane. 'And you can sit down now, Margaret,' she added, 'we'll continue with the Commandment to "honour thy father and thy mother" as that seems appropriate, given the circumstances.'

At that I stole a glance at the dark-haired boy sat in the row behind me. Thomas McGee's black eyes flashed back at me, mirroring my triumph. I smiled at him, the lad from a few streets away who had been my childhood sweetheart since I started school. He was three years older than me, but as our class was made up of a hotchpotch of ages, it was usual for him to be sat nearby, throwing me cheeky smiles and making faces to make me giggle when the nuns weren't looking. His approving grin meant the world to me, and I sat down feeling like a princess, so unused was I to all the attention.

In a moment everyone else had sat down and was bent over their books, heads bowed to the windows, as silent as if nothing at all had happened. But for me, the sounds of the cheering and the bright, happy eyes turned in *my* direction would stay with me, not just for that day, but perhaps for the rest of my life. Of course, I did what I did at home for love of my family. It would never have occurred to me to be thanked for my tasks. But being clapped was another thing entirely. For a moment I had drunk in the admiration, knowing that it would be a memory I would always treasure, one I would come back to on harder days than this, when the job of caring for everyone might feel more like a heavy burden. That day wasn't today, though. Today was a day of wonder, and I savoured every second of it for many, many long days and nights to come.

Thomas met me outside the gates as he usually did, and together with Lizzy Murray and Mary Livingstone, who we called 'Livy', we skipped and chatted our way home. Innocent children buoyed up by the day's unexpected treasures.

Back at our flat, I told Father as we all sat down to dinner. He watched me speak, drinking in my silent words but understanding them as if he could still hear a whisper. His face softened from the hardness of his day's toil, and he nodded, smiling to me, his pride evident for me to see. I drank in his response too, feeling again the love and security that had been in short supply since Mam left. I may have been dog tired, I may have had new blisters on my hands that weren't there even two weeks ago, but I had the love of my dad and it meant the world to me. He'd had a hard life born of the hard lives of generations, and praise for his daughter was a small jewel to be carried close.

Da had nothing to his name. No real treasures except us. His family had come over to Liverpool from Ireland during the famine. Sick and desperate, carrying only few bundles of clothing and food, his relatives, along with many others, came through Clarence Dock Gates into the city to escape the horrors of starvation in their homeland. They hoped for a better life, one free of poverty and hardship. I can't say they found it, looking round at our scant possessions, the smallness of our lives in this dockside slum.

Da's grandparents had arrived on a small fishing boat, hoping to find decent work and a better life for themselves. They'd landed after a treacherous journey across the Irish Sea, and settled in Scotland Road, or Scottie Road as we called it. Their desperation, their privations only attracted more of the same as they became beholden to slum landlords and casual, badly paid work. The security, the bright future they'd longed for, was no more a reality than finding gold at the end of a rainbow. But, they got on with it. They had to.

Cradling babes in arms, they found a place to start anew with at least a crust of bread or a pan of scouse waiting for them at the end of each hard day.

My father was the proof of their willpower, their determination to have more than a starving belly. He had cared for his parents from an early age. His father had been a bare-knuckle fighter, known locally as 'La Riley' and he'd earned extra pennies fighting other dockers and local hard men in the back alleys, while his mother, who was blind, took in home work such as sewing. It was said she could thread a needle using only her tongue! As a result, Thomas was a proud, self-reliant and dignified man with a young family and a sense of duty that kept him shackled to dangerous, hard-bitten work, and he did it for us. He did it because he would no more think of abandoning us in our plight than he would fly to the moon.

Many a young woman with mouths to feed around our way saw her man up and leave for the sake of a prettier skirt or a love for his ale that outweighed that for his family. Families were left to starve and it wasn't unusual. Not ours though. I had seen the determination on Father's face to make sure we carried on as a family as best we could without Mary, the woman who had been our mam, and who I now vowed never to call by the name that spoke so much of love.

Little did I know on that summer evening, as I sat by Da's knee and watched the dying embers of the fire, that I would never see her again. That evening with Father was one that shone through the hard days to come. It was an evening of gentle grace, of tenderness felt among the shock and terror of losing a mother's love. It was a point in time where I felt the full force of my father's affection for me, his quiet love and his fierce duty to keep all of us little ones safe. That night at our bedside prayers, Tommy, Nellie and I prayed for God to forgive Mary, wherever she was, and to give strength and peace to our father. He was the one who needed, and deserved, our thoughts, and we all went to sleep with his name on our lips and hearts.

CHAPTER 3

A Pan of Scouse

November 1932

Heaving the large bundle onto my shoulder I steadied myself, then, grabbing the smaller of the two parcels, I wedged open the front door with my foot. A cacophony of sound greeted me from the teaming street inches from my grimy steps.

It was past noon and the nuns had given me the afternoon off school, as they did every Wednesday, so I could race home and pack up our bedding and clothing into old sheets for me to transport through the din to the Burroughs Garden Bath and Wash House. It wasn't an easy task.

I was already showing the signs of a life spent cooking, cleaning, scrubbing and washing for my family. I had callouses on my hands where there were once ink stains and smut. I had a permanently sore back from bending over to sweep the floors and scrub our front steps. As we lived on the ground floor, it was down to me to clean them. I was determined that none of our neighbours would say we weren't coping without a mother, but it cost me dear.

All the same, I'd never have spoken out about my worries or pains. Da had enough on his plate with finding work, and the 'children', as I now called my younger siblings, even though I was only twelve years old, were busy being young and carefree. Their lives were little changed in a practical sense by Mary's departure. They still had their dinner made, their hair brushed and their clothes washed and ready for school. They still raced through the docklands, collecting the bits of coke that fell out of the coke wagon each day, and playing with a skipping rope strung across the court – where twenty or so of our small court's children could dash in and out to skip to their heart's content.

I loved seeing them play, that was how I wanted it. They didn't deserve to have their world disrupted for the sake of a woman who couldn't love her children enough to stay. No, the work of the house was my duty and mine alone. I would do whatever it took to keep my beloved family clean and fed.

The chill in the damp air greeted me as I stepped gingerly onto Athol Street. It was November and the cold permeated every crevice of our homes and lives. With little enough money to live on for food and warm clothing, we scavenged what we could from the roads for our fires; discarded pieces of coal and tar blocks from the roads. It was never enough to keep us warm and so I looked forward to my wash days, despite the workload, as it was the one place that was always sweltering hot.

I immediately had to dodge the rag-and-bone man calling out, 'Bring me yer jars an' rags,' in his voice made rough by the cheap tobacco he puffed on. He always had a wink for me and a ciggie slumped out of his mouth that stayed in place despite his hollering. Then there were the dockers without work, milling about on our street corners smoking roll-ups, and the coal heavers carrying their shovels on their shoulders, the gossiping housewives cackling with laughter and crossing themselves to sanctify the joke. It was a hive of activity.

The air stank of horse shit and fumes from the gas works, the tang of spices from the docks and the dank vapours from the factories that lined the docksides. Pollution, dirt and industry shaped our streets and its inhabitants, as filthy children ridden with lice and old men in tattered clothing kicked the cobbles and went about their business, scratching out a life for themselves, feeling the permanent pull of hunger that we all felt, however much we worked our fingers to the bone.

I had no time to dwell on this, though, as I only had a couple of hours before the children burst out of school and ran their way home, in a tangle of relief and freedom from a day spent contemplating their prayer books.

Come on, our Maggie, get a move on girl, I said to myself, as I pitched forward into the seething mass of humanity, *ye haven't got all day*. It wasn't too long a walk to the wash house. Indeed I felt myself fortunate to have the brand-new baths to clean our things in, which cost us only two pennies per trip as I carried with me everything I needed. I'd sent Tommy out to the general store on Latimer Street at 9 p.m. last night as we'd run out of Reckitt's Blue. He hurried back with a bar of red carbolic soap, as that was all that could be had amid the piles of products such as pegs, baskets, brooms and coal shovels that the shop's frontage displayed in a higgledy-piggledy mess. The stores round our way were open day and night as we shopped for things as we needed them, there was no thought to stock up as we barely had enough to live on hour by hour some days.

Stepping into the wash house at last, I was hit by a wall of steam and the noise of the chatter of women, as they went about scrubbing and catcalling to each other, their sleeves rolled up to their elbows, hands plunged into hot water frothy with soap suds, their faces red and glistening. I stopped for a moment, caught by the sights and sounds. The big copper boilers gave off the most incredible fiery heat, there was water slopped everywhere in the vast space, and rising above it all were the harmonies of the 'professional' washerwomen, singing as they scoured their mountains of laundry.

I pushed through the door, found a booth with a scrubbing board and gratefully set my bundles down, rubbing my shoulders to try and ease the aching.

'All right, queen, yer arl man works ye hard doesn't he, like?' teased the woman working in the booth next to me.

I smiled in response, grabbing the first of my father's shirts and attacking his greying collar with my brush and carbolic.

'Ye don't talk much, do yer girl?' she continued.

I looked up again. It was one of Mary's drinking pals from the alehouses on Scottie Road. I recognised her because I'd been sent by Da to pull Mary out of them enough times, to remind her she had dinner to cook for her family. I nodded again, wondering if she knew where Mary had gone to, and whether she had known that she was going to abandon us. After all she'd met her fancy man in one of those godforsaken pubs.

The woman was called Cissie and lived in the next court to ours. She had five boys and three girls, and a docker husband who was well known for dragging her through our streets to bring her home to her babies. She would once have been a good-looking woman. She still had long fair hair and pale skin, and a figure that belied her birthing so many children. But the drink and the hardships of her life had worn her into premature ageing. Her skin was coarse, and her manners worse.

I turned back to my washing, hoping Cissie would find another object for her amusement. As I started to scrub furiously, she began to sing a bawdy verse about a sailor and a local girl. I shut my ears to it and carried on, feeling the sweat slide down my back as I heaped wet shirts and vests on top of each other ready for the mangle. The sheets were the worst, carrying them when they were dry was hard enough, but when they were wet from my labours they felt as weighty as sacks Father hauled off the great ships.

'Queen, hold this end of me sheet for me will yer?' shouted Cissie over the din.

My stomach swooped as I realised she meant me. I turned to take hold of the wet sheet that she was holding out to me.

'Now are ye all right, our Maggie? How have yer been coping without yer mam?' Cissie ventured, throwing me a sly look, but with a surprisingly soft voice.

I nodded again, not trusting myself to speak. I didn't want to tell her of all people about my worries.

'It's a hard life, girl, even Our Lady knows that, yes she does. Well I haven't seen yer mam, if that's what yer thinking. I don't hold with what she did, lifting her skirts for another man and running off like that.' Cissie sounded kind, and I looked up at her, tears forming at the back of my eyes, even though it was more than a year since our mother had vanished from our lives.

'We can manage,' was all I said, my voice came out croaky with the suppressed emotion, but she smiled at that, as if she knew and understood.

'Make sure ye can, queen, and if you and yer arl man aren't then there's plenty round here who'll help ye out, don't you forget that.' With that, she threw me a kindly wink and folded up her sheet with the efficiency born of a thousand other times she'd washed, folded and carried her loads.

For a moment I was stunned by her compassion. I'd expected to meet with ... with what? I wasn't even sure. Not this gentleness, especially not from one such as Cissie who enjoyed a scoop of ale too much and moaned loudly to anyone who would listen about 'her John' and how he always spoiled her 'little' bit of fun'. I watched her as she whistled loudly to herself while rubbing a soiled vest, and wondered at the community I lived in. I accepted that everyone knew our business, but I had never really appreciated how that could be a blessing. Her kind words had opened up something inside me that I had shut firmly the day Mary left. I hadn't allowed myself to grieve for her deserting us, there was always too much to do. But it wasn't just that. I was scared that if I let myself cry I might never stop. But this woman, who I barely knew, and who, frankly, I hadn't really warmed to, had shown me kindness, and I suddenly felt exhausted by it, the only true agony being real, unexpected tenderness.

I have to go, I thought to myself, *I mustn't cry in here, like*. With a childlike sob held deep inside me, I quickly sorted our sheets and clothes, Da's vests and shirts, Tommy's shorts and Nellie's dress. I squeezed them between the mangle's great rollers through a blur of wet eyes, then in weepy confusion packed up the lot to carry home.

By now I was tired, and feeling a pain in my heart that I hoped would subside under the mountain of chores I still had to complete before nightfall. I still had Tommy's socks to darn, and the dinner to prepare, so I loaded myself up again, pushed open the big wooden doors that marked our bath house and trudged back home. Black smoke hung over the streets and cobbles, a shopkeeper yelled foul-mouthed insults at a river urchin who grinned and kicked a pebble towards me. The movement of people made me struggle, but finally I made it up our three steps to open the front door and collapse on Da's chair.

The bundles fell to the floor and became instantly covered in the thick dust that could somehow never be swept away. Fresh tears came to me then. I felt suddenly very young and overwhelmed by the cards fate had dealt me. I hadn't yet cried for my mother, but I felt it as keenly today as I had that day sixteen months earlier when the devastating truth of her departure was revealed. The shock, the worry, the hurt of that day flooded through me, and I finally surrendered to the feelings I'd hidden for so long.

Wracked with sobs, I bent my head down to my knees, my arms hugging my thin body and felt the waves of grief and loss shudder through me as my heart poured out into a long, sorrowful lament. I didn't care if anyone heard me, I was too far gone into my despair. Our walls were paper thin so nothing got past our neighbours either in the rooms above or the cellar basement below. I wept until my emotions were spent, leaving me with an empty, hollow feeling.

I wiped the snot from my nose with my arm like the young girl I still was, but vowed silently that I would never cry for Mary again with the fervent passion of a young woman. I'd done with tears. I'd done with pity. She'd gone and there was nothing else for it but to get on with my life, and help my family each day.

It was then that I noticed something. I sniffed the air. It smelled good! I glanced up, scanning the small dingy room with its faded, peeling wallpaper and its black range belching smoke from the fire lit beneath it, to find the source of that seductive scent. The fire was lit! It gave the room a soft heat I hadn't noticed in my distress. I looked round in astonishment, I knew I hadn't left it burning this morning. We'd had bread and water for breakfast as money was tight. I inhaled again. The tantalising smell of something cooking was coming from the pan on the range. I definitely hadn't left anything cooking. *What in the heavens was going on?*

I got up and shuffled to the range, feeling the aches and pains of a much older woman, but I was transfixed. I couldn't believe my eyes. There, on the hob, sat a pan of scouse, the thick hearty stew that gave us Liverpudlians our nick name.

'Go 'ed, how did I miss seein' that!' I exclaimed aloud.

I opened the pan lid to be greeted by the enticing waft of a simmering mass of neeps, spuds and the scrag end of what smelled like lamb bobbing in the brown liquid stock! It was like a miracle.

Quickly, I crossed myself, turning to the statue of Our Lady. Her cool, beatific smile shone back at me, constant and pale, and my hurts and pains melted away. Set against her suffering, her love, my worries seemed feeble, inconsequential.

Just then, before I'd formed a thought in my head in response to this moment of pure beauty, there was a brief knock at the door. It opened to reveal our neighbour from across the court, Mrs Jones, who I never called by her first name, Sarah, as it wasn't considered polite (even though Cissie didn't seem to mind).

'All right our kid? What's all this eh, queen?' Her face swooped from a friendly look to one of concern when she saw my red eyes. She bustled into the room, her faded apron just about stretching round her plump girth. 'Now then, our Maggie, there's no need to cry, the worst is over,' and with that she came straight over to me and pulled me into her arms for the hug I desperately needed, despite my attempts at putting on a brave face for everyone.

I'd cried all my tears, but the solace of those few precious moments meant the world to me. Mrs Jones was always good to us children. She lived directly across the way, her front door being almost opposite ours in the court. She was always at home, a cheery and busy soul who kept her family buoyant with a smile and a kind word. Her old man was a casual docker like Da, and together they'd trudge down to the pen each morning at daybreak to hope they'd be chosen for work. Most days they were picked, and they knew how lucky they were so neither of them wasted the fruits of their toils in the alehouses that stretched from one end of Scottie Road to the other. They were both hard-working, God-fearing, dignified men who loved their families. We knew we were the lucky ones to have men like them; there were plenty who hadn't.

Despite her continual good cheer, Mrs Jones bore the unmistakeable signs of an impoverished life. It couldn't be helped. With a new child every year and a life of feeding babies, soaking and scrubbing nappies, and the constant effort to make ends meet, she looked a good deal older than her thirty-five years. With wispy brown hair, and a permanent set of lines above her forehead, she looked like she worked as hard as she did from dawn till dusk. Her stockings were always wrinkled, her apron not the cleanest, but her spirit was undaunted. I'd never heard a word of complaint pass her smiling lips. She always had a twinkle in her eye when she saw us children, even the occasional boiled sweet to give us if times were good. We all loved her. She was the heart and soul of our court and often it was her that women, and sometimes even their men, turned to for a word of good, sound advice.

When Father worked late at the docks, she'd regularly take us in and give us whatever she'd managed to rustle up to fill all those empty bellies. With a baby latched on the breast, she'd dole up ladles of thick scouse, leaning between the lines of drying nappies strung across the small kitchen that dripped dolefully onto our meals. Or she'd scrape a mouthful of jam, all that she could spare, to make butties to keep us going until Father returned from work with something for the pot. Those jam butties became a thing of wonder, a welcome snack to tide us over, and proof, if any were needed, that we were as much part of her family as her own squalling infants.

Later in life as a wife and mother, I too dished out those simple sandwiches to my own offspring, and they were always eaten with relish. In many ways, Mrs Jones had been a surrogate mother to us even when Mary was still there. Her kindness and simple, open-hearted spirit was a contrast to the many difficulties of our lives; the cold, the hunger and the lack of a mother's nurturing love.

Once I'd pulled out of Mrs Jones' embrace, she held me at arm's length. 'Ye need some colour in them cheeks, girl. Come on, our Maggie, there's a pan of scouse waiting for ye all for tonight. Ye won't go hungry, and if there's any left ye keep it fer tomorrow, ye hear me?'

I nodded, barely able to speak, my gratitude and affection for her was so strong.

'There's proper food in there so no need to cry. Me arl fella and yours have got a day's work under their belts today so you won't be skint come Friday payday. There'll be money in the pot so no more tears, it's not all bad, girl!'

With that Mrs Jones waggled a finger at me, and I laughed my response. 'Thank ye,' was all I managed to say.

'That's all right, queen, ye get yerself a proper meal inside you and ye won't feel so bad.' Our kindly neighbour beamed.

She was expecting another baby to join the other four she

had round her tiny table that night. She'd always said to me that 'babbies' were a blessing sent from 'Jaysus' so there was no point in complaining when there were miracles aplenty in our lives. She was as devout a Catholic as I knew. Her faith lit her way through her hardships. Neither she nor Mr Jones ever missed Mass on Sundays, and she went most days as well, handing her suckling babe to another housewife in the court and busying off with combed hair and without the customary apron that every woman in our area seemed to wear morning, noon and night. I would watch her go most days, and envied her her freedom. More and more I had turned to Our Lady for strength and support through days when I thought I was so weary I couldn't go a step further. She always shone a small light in my soul, and reminded me that our traditions and faith were the backbone of our meagre existence.

I never questioned our religion. It was the only real constant in lives that were spent ducking and diving to survive each and every day. Every Friday when Da was paid, I'd go down to the pawn shop to retrieve his best, and only, suit so that he'd have it for church on Sunday, and sometimes even his shoes as well, which he'd have cleaned and polished before handing to the pawnbroker for a few extra pennies to tide us through the week. It was part of our ritual. Collect the clobber and make sure we were all spick and span, ready to shake the hand of the priest at St Anthony's Church on Scotland Road, where we attended Mass without fail every week. I could not conceive of a life without our church, without the prayers that whispered our hopes and dreams, our failures and our deprivations. The priest's billowing, colourful robes, the waft of the incense, taking communion and going to confession, these were the threads that wove together the fabric of our lives. Without them I would be lost.

Every Sunday we'd head to the church to stand in the Poor Ground, the space at the back where the priest, sensitive to our financial plight, would not pass the collection box. After the service, we always felt lighter, like we weren't the offspring of slum dwellers and casual labourers, but in fact we were all children of God and we were blessed.

I mused on this as I folded up the washing to take out into the cold of the yard. Washing lines were strung between the buildings in the court, set against the partly whitewashed walls, which had been an earlier attempt to brighten up the hovel we lived in. Money had run out and the white paint stopped just above door level, but it made a small difference. I hopped over a puddle formed of the scum of non-existent drains, and set my basket down. Holding the wooden pegs in my mouth, I hummed as I worked, pinning the clothing including our knickers and vests, out in the street for all to see. It was how things were done. We didn't have the room inside so everything had to go out there, in its fraying, greying glory.

Time and time again, I counted myself lucky to have been born a Scouser. The people of my beloved city, and especially those whom I lived among in these desperate streets, proved to be my salvation. There was no community in the world like ours. We might have our problems, and our fights, we might judge each other harshly for liking the beer or arguing with a spouse, but at the end of the day we all kept each other alive. After all, there was no one else out there who would. There were no handouts except in the form of food parcels and day trips from bodies like the cherished League of Welldoers. We had each other, and we each had nothing, so the ties that bound us together were tight as only those of the destitute could be.

In one day I'd been doubly blessed with the kindness of

friends and strangers. Despite the biting cold, I smiled as I hung the last of the clothes, gathered the remaining pegs up and looked to the heavens, saying a silent prayer of gratitude.

CHAPTER 4

Ferry Across the Mersey

Spring–summer 1933

'Go 'ed, yous two, get yerselves off to school!' I grinned at Tommy and Nellie as I flapped a drying sheet at them before finishing the dishes.

Tommy chuckled as he grabbed his flat cap from the table. 'Can't catch me, our Nellie!' said the boy of ten who looked more like our father Thomas every day.

With that, he pocketed an apple from the bowl sat next to his hat, and throwing me a cheeky glance he whistled as he sauntered out of the kitchen. Fair-haired Nellie reached up to me for a quick kiss and a cuddle before leaving the home for her lessons. Just five years old, Nellie was the sweetest little girl on our street. People always commented what a pair of beauties we made when we were out together, popping to one of the shops for a small quantity of lard or picking up yet more soap. I would blush at the compliments, which were always well-intentioned, but Nellie would accept them gravely, with a serious nod, which slowly turned into the prettiest smile for miles around. I bent down to draw Nellie into my embrace. Her curls smelt of carbolic and I felt my heart swell with love and pride as I hugged her. She lifted up her little lips for a sloppy kiss, which she then wiped away with the back of her hand.

'Eh, our Tommy, wait up fer yer sister!' I shouted out of the front door, laughing at the sight of my brother's cheeky face as he kicked his heels on the cobbles.

The day was bright, as much as it could be under the

layers of smog and fumes our thriving industries belched out each day, but spring had finally arrived, and even the hint of sunlight brightened the mood of us slum dwellers. There was nothing like seeing the end of winter, the finish of those cold, hard-bitten days for another year, for making my soul soar. But, despite the fun we were having, I too had to get to class, or I'd feel the lash of the nun's ruler on my knuckles! *Get a move on, girl*, I said to myself, as I swept up the crumbs from breakfast and rinsed out the plates and tea cups in the scullery. *Mustn't forget to pass by the butcher's on me way home tonight, see if there isn't something fer a few pennies fer the pot.*

I made a mental note of all the chores I still had to complete by the end of day as I pulled a comb through my rich brown hair and pulled off Mary's old apron. Looking at myself in the cracked mirror that hung by the front door, I saw my bright blue eyes staring back at me, winking like diamonds as I smiled at myself. Life wasn't all bad – even if I was late for class and got beaten for missing morning prayers. I grabbed an apple for later, smoothed down my dress and ran out of the flat, jumping down the steps I had brushed and scrubbed only yesterday evening. I loved school. It was the only place that I got to be a child again. I loved reading my prayer book and being taught the lessons it had for us, as well as hearing the Bible stories set in far-off lands. My life felt so small in comparison, yet I was happy. I had a loving father, and two adorable siblings who I treasured.

On days like this, I would say we thrived, against all the odds, all the things that could so easily have beaten us, such as the rats, the lice, the childhood diseases and stillbirths that were the curse of our community. *Here we all were, and here we'll probably stay*, I thought to myself as I skipped down to the end of our street to meet with my best friend, Lizzy Murray.

Lizzy was the beauty of our school. She had the fair skin of the Irish settlers and long, dark hair. We'd shared a joke or two in class and now we were firm friends. Each morning, after I'd finished my chores, I'd race to her house, which was at the 'posh' end of our street, unlike our family down 'over the bridge', which was the poorest, yet most close-knit end of Athol Street. Lizzy had a 'proper' family; a mother and a father who with every gesture showed how in love they were with each other. They lived in a few rooms, not dissimilar to ours, but her father was on a regular wage as a dock manager and so their home was like a palace compared to ours, or that's how I saw it.

Each morning, I'd stop to catch my breath, pull myself up so I looked as respectable as possible, tidying my dress to hide the creases, then I'd knock. Lizzy's mam would open the door and give me a nice smile, and always ask me how I was doing. She'd usher me into the first of the small rooms, and even when I'd been there dozens of times, I caught my breath being surrounded by such luxuries as a proper settee, a wireless and net curtains at the windows!

I'd never let Lizzy come to my home. House-proud as I was, I never felt confident enough to show her our rickety wooden table and three old wooden chairs that surrounded it, the greying walls and old iron bed that made up the sum of our possessions. It wasn't that I was ashamed of us, how could I be? I saw how hard Da worked each day. It was that I didn't want anything to break the spell of my new-found feelings of security and safety with him at the helm, fighting against circumstances bigger than ourselves. No, I didn't want a casual word, or a repressed shudder to show me our poverty in its reality. Of course, I made excuses every time Lizzy wanted to see our home, saying Father wasn't back, or Tommy was ill, but really, I just wanted to stay in our bubble of happy friendship which nothing, no old tin bath or shared lavvy, could burst.

When Lizzy had put on her beret and smiled her lovely smile, we'd link arms and chatter excitedly all the way to St Sylvester's School, arriving seconds before the first prayers of the day. At school we'd meet with our other friend Livy, or Mary Livingstone. She also lived close by and loved to share a joke and a laugh together, sometimes even at the expense of the nuns! Livy was dark-haired and slim, with a sunny personality and a cheeky laugh. The three of us would sit together, whispering in lessons and giggling to ourselves, even when our teacher was reciting the Ten Commandments. At break time we'd huddle together, sharing secrets and creating little worlds for ourselves, far away from the harsh realities of our streets.

They were happy days, despite the fact that money was tight, and when it came to home-time, Lizzy and I linked arms to wander off together for a few precious hours before ambling home at twilight. I would savour each moment as we drew nearer, dawdling to eke out every last second of her company and dreading the start of my evening's chores. We'd pass the lamplighters, cast in the orange glow of the gas lights' flame, and small knots of grubby boys shouting 'Heads a dollar' as they tossed ha'pennies and caught them in their small fists. The dusk would hover at our heels, despite it being not long after 6 p.m. The horses and carts with their advertising boards trotted by, leaving piles of steaming dung behind them.

Eventually, I could tarry no longer, and I'd wave goodbye to Lizzy as she stepped into her house, then sigh as I turned to face our end of the road. With a nod from Mary Ellen the washerwoman sitting on her steps smoking a ciggie, and a wink from John the coalman making his rounds, I'd continue home, finally ready to resume my role as our family's makeshift mother. Yawning, I'd pull on my apron, see what my father had left us for the pot, and set the spuds on to boil.

Tonight there was only a bit of barley, some turnips and an onion to throw in, but it was dinner at least, and we'd all welcome something hot in our bellies before nightfall. Tommy appeared with Nellie a few moments later, leaving his charge with me and instantly dashing outside again to play football with his pals in the court. He'd be out until it was too dark to play, chasing round the streets with an abandon I envied. Nellie sat at the table as I worked, chattering about her day, when there was a sharp rap on the door.

Who can that be, like? I thought to myself, wiping my hands on Mary's apron and heading to the door.

'Go 'ed, queen, no need to look so shocked, it's only me. What can I do for ye this week, girl?' John the coalman doffed his flat cap to me, and our Nellie. He was always a proper gent.

'Too much on me mind, our John,' I laughed, reaching behind me for the jar with the shillings and pennies that Father gave me each week for the housekeeping.

Da earned twenty-eight shillings a week, and almost half of that went on our rent so there was never much to spare.

'Any coal for ye? Yer've gorra keep yer bones warm!' John smiled, not looking at the poor offering I was preparing as our only hot meal of the day.

I blushed. 'Well, I don't know about that, but the weather's turnin' fer the better so I won't be needin' much of yer wares today, John,' I replied. Coal was expensive and as I looked at the small selection of coins in my hand I frowned. 'Perhaps we'll just have a bag or two of coke, instead, as it's warmer, like,' I stammered, flushed with the shame of our poverty.

'Two bags of coke it is, girl, and don't ye worry, better times are comin',' smiled John kindly.

'Oh, so you can read fortunes can ye?' I giggled, grateful for his sympathy. I couldn't hide our circumstances, but knowing I wasn't judged for it made things feel a little better, at least.

'I surely can,' joked the coalman, whose face was as black as those exotic fellas down at the dockside, the ones with skin burnt the colour of molasses. He paused to wipe a smut from his eye as he chortled, 'You, girl, are goin' to have a long and happy life. I swear it, ye mind my words.'

With that he beamed again before backing out of the doorway, returning seconds later with the first of the two bags that would keep our range burning and our tea hot for the rest of the week. He heaved the second sack inside, placing it carefully next to the range, then with another tip and a wink he departed. I could hear his cheery whistle as he went off down the street, back to his handcart.

Just then, Da's heavy tread sounded on the front steps. His way of walking was unmistakeable as he still limped from his old injuries. Just from hearing the sound of his footsteps, I could guess at the tiredness he felt after his twelve hours hauling freight amid the chaos and dangers of the docks and its ships.

'All right, queen, how's yous all?' smiled Thomas as he entered our small kitchen.

Nellie jumped up from her chair and ran to greet him, burying her soft face into his dirt-encrusted jacket.

'Well, aren't ye a sight for sore eyes, eh girl,' Da said softly, enclosing her in the bulk of his stocky frame. 'And how's about our Maggie, eh?'

He wouldn't be able to hear our answers so I let my grin speak for me. He was the best father a girl could wish for, a humble man whose only treasures were his three children and the Dockers Union Badge he wore proudly in his lapel on his best, and only, suit every Sunday. He was a simple man, devoted to providing for his family with a sense of duty that saw he never complained about his lot in life. I never once heard him say a bad word about Mary, our mam, despite the hurt and bewilderment he must have felt at her betrayal of their marriage vows, or about the hardships and toils he faced every day of his life.

Thomas Riley had married Mary Mullen at the grand old age of thirty-three. He had lied about his age to Mary, who was eleven years younger than her husband, saying that he was eight years' younger than he really was so that she'd accept his proposal. They married on August 2nd, 1916 at St Mary of the Angels Church in Fox Street, Everton, and started married life as happy as two people could be. That was, until it became clear that Mary liked a few too many scoops of ale, and spent more time than was good for her down in the many pubs that lined Scottie Road in those days, more than 200 of them at the time. My father's accidents at work might have been the trigger for Mary to look elsewhere, but who could say? She was still young, only thirty-six when she left us, more than enough time to start again if she wished. Da never spoke another word about Mam after that conversation telling us she'd gone, and I didn't dare ask him anything more as I knew he felt things deeply. His pride must have been deeply wounded, as was his heart.

The young girl that I was, I wanted to talk about her; about why she left and how I felt, but I could see my father retreating into himself more and more, becoming closed off to us in his sorrow. So I never asked him, or reproached him for his unwillingness to talk. He had us, and we loved him with a fierce devotion. Our neighbours had pitched in, gifting us their hand-me-down clothes, bringing us a pan of scouse now and then, or feeding us those jam butties when we went short, but he did the best he could.

'Now then, our Maggie, ye lookin' tired, girl, ye need a treat so you do.' Da said, scratching his chin and pulling his thick hands through his work-soiled hair.

'Go 'ed, Da, where would we get the money fer a treat? I'm happy enough, I don't need anythin',' I replied firmly, and quite loudly, so that he could get the gist of what I was saying as I doled out ladles of hot stew into our chipped plates. 'Now, get that inside ye,' I finished. 'Tommy, Nellie, dinner's on the table!'

Nellie and Tommy prattled their childlike stories through our meal. I glanced over at Da but he was already looking at me, a quizzical expression on his face.

'Go 'ed, Father, eat up while it's hot. I'm fine, I promise, never happier.' I couldn't help but let a small sigh escape my lips. I was tired, in fact I was exhausted, but I didn't want that to add to his worries.

After we'd finished eating, I got up to rinse the plates, and he held out a hand to stop me. Nellie and Tommy had wiggled out of their chairs and had trotted off into the bedroom. Silently, Da reached into his pocket and drew out two pennies, carefully placing them on the table. I watched him, wondering where this was leading.

I knew we had no money to spare, only last week we'd had to accept a handout from the nice ladies of the League of Welldoers, a gift of foodstuffs given to tide over the poorest. The shame of it burnt in my heart, but I wasn't so proud I couldn't accept a bit of charity when the alternative was a sore belly. I'd also been forced to borrow half a crown from the moneylenders a few weeks ago who haunted our parish of 'Silly' (our name for St Sylvester's), so that Tommy could have a pair of shorts and Nellie a new dress. I was paying it back at three shillings interest a week, a small fortune to the likes of us, and I hadn't told Da. I couldn't bear to see his shame at not being able to support his family properly. So why then were there two gleaming coins sat on the table?

'This is for ye, our Maggie. I won't hear a word against it, I've made up me mind. I had a bit of luck earning some extra shifting some of the bigger sacks and I want ye to have it.' My da stopped talking and pushed the coins towards me.

'I can't take them, Da.' I looked up at his kind, solid face and I could see that my words were literally falling on deaf ears. He could see my response, not hear it, and it made no difference.

'Yer've always wanted to go on them ferries across the Mersey, so this is what this is for. I won't hear another word from ye about it.' And with that, my father scraped his chair away from the table and turned to face the burning embers of the cooking fire, retreating back into his customary silence.

I knew I couldn't argue with him, and I can't deny that my heart had lit up at the sight of those two small tickets to freedom and adventure for the day. The thought of a trip on the high waters that framed our city made my heart swell. I looked back at Da, to make sure he was serious and hadn't changed his mind. He sat staring at the orange flames, deep in thought. Carefully I placed the money in the palm of my hand. This was my money, *my* money! At first I felt guilty, it seemed wrong not to use the money to pay off the moneylenders. I looked over at Da, who was gazing at the fire intently. I realised he would never forgive me if I didn't allow him to treat me. I couldn't disappoint Da. I couldn't rob him of this moment. I smiled and nodded. He looked over at me, registering my acceptance, ruffled his hair and shifted back in his chair, looking as content as I'd ever seen him. Feeling like I'd won the Littlewood Pools, I had a rush of happiness. I would take Lizzy on Saturday afternoon after I'd done my chores. I could almost taste the fresh, wind-whipped freedom on my tongue. A trip on the Mersey!

Saturday came at last. I spent the week fidgeting with impatience. More than once I got my knuckles rapped at school for not paying proper attention. Eventually the great day arrived. I was up earlier than usual, scrubbing, sweeping and cleaning, peeling spuds and getting everything ready for my family so I wouldn't have to work later.

Lizzy and I arranged to meet at midday. We ran and laughed like two caged birds suddenly freed to swoop and plane through the teaming streets. Leaping onto a tram, we giggled as it swayed down Scottie Road towards the waterfront, where we leapt off to duck and weave in and out of the crowds to find Liverpool's famous Pier Head Ferry Terminal. The terminal was teeming with people, all dressed in their Sunday best, promenading and queuing to get onto the short pier that led to the side of the steam-driven ferry.

Once we'd paid our money and grabbed our tickets in our hands, we shrieked with excitement and found a space on the rail looking over the churning grey water below us. The wind was salty and fresh. It tore at our hair and we laughed with the sheer joy of it. The ferry filled up, people jostling and elbowing their way to the railings, looking down at the people in the berth below and whistling, catcalling and hollering to loved ones on the shore. It was a thrilling spectacle.

With a great bellow, the air was suddenly filled with dense black smoke, the waters beneath our feet foaming as the vessel began to move away from the pier side. Lizzy and I whooped with laughter, a lifelong ambition of mine was about to be realised. Of course I saw the long sweep of our famous river daily, living within spitting distance, but it wasn't until I was riding on it that I realised how vast, how immense it really was. It became something else, a new landscape to experience and by golly we were determined to enjoy each and every second of our big journey!

'Go 'ed, our Lizzy, look if it isn't them liver birds, don't they look small from over here!' I exclaimed, as the ferry chugged off, slowly at first, then gathering pace.

Lizzy gave a long whistle. 'I can't wait to tell me arl man about this,' she crowed, shielding the sunlight from her eyes as she stared back at the receding statues that sat on top of the two towers of the Royal Liver Building, one facing to sea, the other inland. Legend had it that if the two birds were ever to fly off then the city of Liverpool would cease to exist. Well, I didn't know about that, and I couldn't see how two great metal birds could take wing and fly, but as a symbol of my city they looked protective, impressive.

We'd decided we wouldn't get off at the Birkenhead ferry berths at Woodside, we would carry on round and back to Liverpool Landing Stage. We both had jobs to do at home, we knew we couldn't be long, but even so the trip would take the best part of two hours, we reckoned. Plenty of time to find our sea legs and drink in the sights.

'Don't the city look grand,' I shouted over the hubbub of the engine and the crowds.

Lizzy nodded. We were both a little star-struck seeing our native Liverpool from afar. Our daily lives were concerned with the minutiae, the details of domestic life; which buttons to sew, choosing the vegetables to clean and peel, the smut to wipe off dirty cheeks. Seeing our birthplace from a different perspective suddenly made the world feel a bigger place. I shuddered even though the day was quite warm, the river breezes fresh rather than cold.

For once, I had a sense of our city being the trading post it was, how the river drew from three streams; the Goyt, the Etherow and the Tame, and how these three water sources became the moving ferment of a river that linked us to America and beyond. I squinted back at the structures lining the landing stage in the distance, the Royal Liver Building and, next to it, the Cunard Building. For a moment I felt almost dizzy, as if I was a foreigner in my own homeland.

The ferry sliced through the water and we watched as twice it unburdened itself of passengers, people busying off to their work or homes. At this point we'd stopped chatting, and instead gazed at this new land across the river, and the sight of the well-dressed gents and their ladies disembarking next to the street hawkers and coal men. As we left Woodside and headed back to our side of the Mersey, I felt reflective. I was happy, I was loved, but today I'd realised, I think for the first time, that there was another world out there if only we could grasp it.

By now the afternoon was drawing in, and the river breeze felt cold. The wind whipped the water into white tips and it was soon our turn to disembark. Turning to look at the boat, its great funnel pointing up into the sky, the people streaming from inside its bowels, we both sighed. It had been an incredible experience, though different to the one I'd imagined.

It wasn't until twilight fell that Lizzy and I returned home. I could hardly believe that I'd finally been on that great swathe of water that defined our homeland and its place in the world, its connections to trade and industry across the globe. I felt I'd experienced my diverse, far-reaching city in a new way, and in a way that begged of me: What will my place be in that world? Will I ever see those lands beyond our famous stretch of water?

It had been a thrilling adventure, yet the rich cross-fertilisation of peoples from different places, creeds and religions wasn't always such a peaceful fusion, and didn't always sit as happily together as those two great liver birds did. Later that year, as the annual 12th of July parade by the Orangemen approached, tensions simmered, as they did every year, between the Proddys (our word for the Protestants) and Catholics. The houses and streets around Scottie Road were predominantly Catholic Irish immigrant families, and the Orange walk every year that passed through the area created a ripple of sectarian unrest that divided our city across the age-old battle lines of faith and community. Each year, the Orangemen would walk with banners, a great swell of people commemorating the Battle of the Boyne of 1690, for several Sundays in the lead-up to the main parade on the 12th.

Da had warned us not to go, but the urge to scamper through the streets to see the thousands of people who marched through our area, the colour of the banners and sounds of the drumbeats, was too much for us children. We waited until he had put on his Sunday best suit and pinned his Dockers' Union badge on his faded lapel, and left to go to join the other proud Catholic men of our area to line the streets in uneasy witness, before we made our own way.

The cobbled streets were teaming with people. Even though it was an event that marked the deep divisions within our community, at first there was a festival air to the spectacle. Drinking in the sights and sounds, I wove through the crowds, gripping Nellie's hand tightly, following the back of Tommy's head. There was a feeling of excitement, a heady atmosphere, almost as if we were the ones marching! And for a while the crowds stayed friendly enough, the people passed through, staring straight ahead as if all those watching were just a ghostly presence.

I don't know where the first signs came from that things were turning ugly, as Da had predicted. Perhaps a shout from one of the women hanging out of the tennie windows, perhaps an insult thrown from the crowds that were three or four people deep either side of the road. Whatever it was, things quickly spiralled into chaos. There was a scream from some of the marching children dressed in their best clothes, and I craned my neck over the old woman stood in front of me and saw a girl with her clothes streaked black.

'Them's'll be the soot and pepper they're throwin' on those devils,' shouted the woman, glee apparent in her voice.

Tommy edged in front, elbowing her aside to see what was going on. The crowd started to sway and I felt Nellie's hand slip a little from mine. 'Hold on, our Nellie, if we're separated just make for home, d'you hear me?'

I glanced at Nellie's white face. She looked as scared as I

felt. Things felt like they were fast running out of control and we were too far inside the crowd to make an easy escape. 'Don't worry, Nellie, we'll be fine. Just keep hold of me, girl, and Tommy'll keep us safe,' I shouted, not at all sure I was telling the truth.

There was another scream, this time from one of the women in the march. Her clothes were smeared brown, and from her lips erupted a torrent of swear words I could not bring myself ever to repeat.

'Them's throwin' shit on them!' A man's yell rose up from the crowd, delight clearly sounding in his voice.

I could hardly believe it. My neighbours and locals were throwing human excrement at those poor people in the march! However much I was a Catholic and proud of my faith, I still felt sorry for those people being waged war on, undergoing a battery of assault with soot, pepper and worse. All at once a cheer rose up from the crowds and there was a surge forward.

'Nellie! Don't let go!' I screamed, as her hand slipped from mine. 'Tommy! Nellie!' I shouted, beside myself with fear.

The crowd moved again, accompanied by jeers and scuffles nearer the roadside. It was time to go, but I had to find my brother and sister. Pushing through the people with unashamed urgency, I breathed hard, panting with fear. More shouts, more screams. A fight broke out a few feet away and the crowd jostled and catcalled. People seethed around me. The intricately woven banners held aloft over our heads were swaying as the marchers and the crowds merged into unholy confusion.

'Our Nellie, our Tommy!' I hollered again above the raging torment, an elbow poking me, a body shoving roughly against me. My shin was scraped by a stumble from a young lad next to me. I could smell the excrement, the sweat from the spectators and hear the shouts and scrabble as people moved towards the marchers. I felt trapped. I couldn't relish the attacks on the Proddys, even though I was a good Catholic girl. I hated seeing, and hearing, the derision from both sides, Orangemen and Catholics alike. Neither side came out well in my eyes. All I wanted to do now was get to the safety of my home with my family intact, but I couldn't see my sister or my brother.

With a strangled sob I lurched forwards, almost losing a shoe, and with heartfelt relief I spotted Nellie. She was stood in between two women who were shouting and pointing, hurling curses at the Proddies. Nellie was wailing, her hands held tightly over her ears, trying to block out the terrible sounds. With a thrust through the bodies, I grabbed Nellie's arm and fought my way with her through the people. I kept going, the sounds and jeers growing fainter with each step. My heart ceased its pounding, but I didn't stop until we reached Latimer Street and we could lean against the tenements and breathe again.

'Our Nellie, I thought I'd lost you, I'm so sorry, we should never have gone,' I wept, clutching her to me in a tight embrace.

'Ouch, our Maggie, yer hurting me,' replied my little sister, wriggling out of my arms.

Just then Tommy appeared. His cap was gone, but he was grinning and I flew into his arms, crying harder, if that was possible. 'Our Tommy, yer safe!' was all I could say, wiping my tears from my eyes.

'Don't you cry, our Maggie, I'm fine, let's go home.' Tommy said, linking us both in his arms and guiding us back home with a firm grip.

'We mustn't tell Da,' I pleaded to him.

Tommy stepped back, took a long look at me and barked

with laughter. 'Don't know how yer goin' to hide it, look at you!' he exclaimed. I looked down at myself. There were streaks of soot from that hurled by the onlookers.

There was a rip in my skirt and a big purple and yellow bruise already blooming on my ankle. I looked back at Tommy and we both started giggling. Once we started we couldn't stop. Nellie was soon joining us, clutching her sides as we laughed with the immense relief of children saved from a terrible fate. There was nothing more important than the fact we were all together, even if we had some explaining to do to our father that evening.

With a sigh, we all clasped hands again and continued on our way, vowing never again to witness the march that proved so provocative and bloodthirsty. The sea of hatred that transformed our communities into war zones almost engulfed us that day, and I wished that life could always be as simple in its pleasures as it was that day on the ferry across the Mersey.

CHAPTER 5

Lipstick, Powder and Paint

1934–35

'Now then, our Maggie, our Lizzy. No talking in the back!'

The nun shot us both a sharp look, and we giggled our response in unison: 'Sorry Sister.'

That earned us another reproving glance, but today we didn't care. It was our final day at school, the last day we'd ever spend listening to our teacher and her admonishments, the last time we'd risk getting a beating for the sake of a wrong answer or cheeky retort, but it was also the last time we'd sit together, hunched over our work, scribbling secret messages to each other and trying not to laugh over our 'in' jokes.

I'd loved my time at St Sylvester's School and cherished my lessons and learning. It had been the only place that I'd not had to worry about my chores, or about how to make my housekeeping money last for the rest of the week. But I was now a young woman of fourteen, and even though I knew leaving school would only mean yet more housework, yet more motherly duties for me, I was eager to fly the nest and start the next phase of my life.

Lizzy and I smothered our sniggers as Livy nudged my elbow and grinned at us, sharing the joy in our day of 're-lease'. I can't say I was sorry to see the back of some of those nuns. They'd been kind to us, in their way, but I was growing into a confident young woman, and the sight of them in their plain garments and with their strict routines made me yearn even harder for some kind of independence.

Most girls would be going out and getting work in the months to come, but not me. I couldn't see how Da would cope if I was out working all day. There'd be no one to draw the water from the outdoor pump each morning, no one to light the range and make the porridge, no one to scrub the steps, wash the clothes and mend the holes in our outfits. No, I knew that I had no choice but to accept my fate, don Mam's apron for good, and hope that I didn't go crazy with frustration in the process.

Walking out of the school gates for the last time, I turned back to look at the red-brick building that had seen me through my girlhood. With my arms linked into Lizzy on one side and Livy on the other, I bade a silent farewell and suddenly felt a strange terror, the panic of a child who is unsure of the way home. Tears pricked my eyes. I blinked, not realising that I'd felt safe away from the unknown perils and joys of life outside of its thick walls. It wasn't really a new start for me. It was a return to everything that was ordinary, keeping home and hearth together through difficult times. I almost cried out then with that sensation, a sudden fear that this was it for me, this was all I would ever accomplish and my life would be as restricted in future as it had ever been.

Lizzy must have known how I was feeling, or guessed at the anguish behind my eyes, as she whispered to me, 'Time to go, our Maggie, time to go home, girl.'

I turned to her and smiled, then we began the familiar walk that we'd made every day together, rain or shine. We dawdled along Latimer Street, past the soot-blackened tenements, with their black iron railings and men in flat caps loitering outside the baccy shop, until we reached Athol Street, where I turned to go over the bridge and Lizzie took her leave, turning instead to go up the other end, to her nicer house and the prospect of a job perhaps and a future of her own. Livy had turned off at Slade Street, waving goodbye as if we were leaving forever, even though we lived so close by and would no doubt bump into each other as we performed our daily tasks.

Lizzy knew me so well. She looked at my pale face and smiled a reassuring smile. 'Don't you go frettin', our Maggie, it'll all turn out in the end, yer'll see.'

With that, she squeezed my hand in a familiar gesture of reassurance, then slipped away into her new life, while I turned, emitting a soft, desolate sigh, and headed back to mine.

Once in the door I spotted Mam's apron hanging on the nail by the door. I walked slowly over to it and unhooked it, holding the fabric to my face and sniffing it, trying to find a trace of the woman who abandoned us. It smelt of wood smoke and gravy. Mary was long gone, and it was finally my turn to permanently wear the cloth that would meld me into the life that had been waiting for me since I was a mere girl of ten.

I wiped away a tear as I pulled the faded flowery thing around my slim waist and tied it at the back. The transformation was complete. Even though I'd been a surrogate mother for my siblings for over three years and I'd worn her apron most days, something felt different today, more permanent, more unsettling. The question hovered nearby, asking, *Will I ever be free to live my own life?* I mused on this as I pulled up a wooden chair and sat down to peel the spuds and carrots I'd set aside for tonight's stew. My bones felt heavy, the fluttering of an imminent migraine brooding at the back of my neck.

It was no different from any other night: Da was yet to appear after a day's long labour, Tommy and Nellie were out in the streets larking about with their pals, playing alley-o or with a bag of 'ollies (marbles), and I was here, making dinner. Nothing had changed, yet everything had. I felt I had become my mam entire. I had dissolved into the stain she had left behind in these rooms, the imprint of her existence left for me, and only me, to fill. It felt sore, this enclosed space. This enclosed existence. This tatty old apron was the symbol of my tethered flight into womanhood, and from that second onwards I resented it, and resented the circumstances that meant I could not choose to shake off my destiny as easily as untying the apron strings.

Before we knew it we had got through another winter, another Christmas doing the best we could just like all the other families living on the breadline. Father had managed to work through the festivities and so we had a hearty Christmas dinner and even an orange and a penny in our stockings.

At last the days were becoming longer and brighter as spring approached. One day, there was a hurried knock on the door and it burst open to reveal my friend Lizzie. I had only recently told her where we lived, I'd been so ashamed of our humble home. I stood up so fast I forgot I had a pile of socks I was darning on my lap. They peeled to the floor as I moved to exclaim my surprise. Her face was flushed and she looked alive with delight.

'Yer'll never guess, queen, but I'm goin' to be a workin' girl. I've got meself a job!'

In that moment I saw a bright, lively young woman with a future ahead of her. I almost gagged with envy, but I swallowed down my reflex and showed Lizzy my usual, happy smile. 'Go on, our Lizzy, what is it? I'm dyin' here with excitement!'

I bounced over to my friend and grabbed her hands. Her beautiful green eyes were wide. I searched her face, feeling ashamed of myself for my jealousy. I couldn't wish for a better person to have this new start, whatever it was.

'I'm goin' to be a Pendleton's Ices girl! Oooh our Maggie I'm so chuffed, so I am. A proper job, with wages an' me mammy says I can keep back a shilling or two fer meself, get meself a lippie or a pot of powder.'

We were squealing with excitement. A lipstick or a powder puff, how grown up she'd be! Together we danced around the kitchen before collapsing in a giggling heap onto the chairs.

'Make me a cuppa then, girl, she said cheekily, eyeing the cracked cups on the shelf.

I noticed her looking and blushed, but I wasn't going to spoil her day so I jumped up, pretending not to see her concern at our few possessions, and busied myself making a nice hot cup of tea.

'We've got no milk,' I said, not turning my head so she couldn't see my blush deepen.

'Don't drink it with milk, anyway,' she replied straight away, the lie coming easily to her lips to spare my feelings.

We blew on the steaming drinks, and I listened to my best friend prattle away about her job. She'd been for an interview up at the factory in Kirkby, taking a bus by herself and queuing up with the other girls wanting work. She'd been seen there by a very stern shop floor manager, and given a medical to make sure she was fit and healthy.

'An' they're givin' me a uniform. I'm made up about it,' she added, grinning from ear to ear. 'My job'll be to put the sticks in the lollies, and I might even do some packing. It isn't the best work, I won't be in the office, like, but who knows where it may lead, eh, queen?'

We both laughed at that.

After Lizzy had left I sat for a moment, a small shaft of sunlight lighting my face as it came through the small, grimy kitchen window. Outside in the court I could see grey washing hanging in bedraggled lines and a seagull pecking at the stone flags on the ground. Perhaps I would never know Lizzy's freedom. Perhaps I would never get a job of my own. Yet even though I envied Lizzy sorely, I couldn't help but feel glad for her good fortune. And it was good fortune, to us. We knew we were factory girls in the making. We didn't aspire to anything higher than that. We were happy with a few coins in our purse and a good natter with our friends. How could I begrudge my oldest friend that happiness?

I turned to Our Lady, who smiled in creamy solitude as the last rays of light outlined her small figure. I smiled to myself, feeling strangely content, feeling that all was well in the world, even though nothing had yet changed for me.

A few weeks later, as I was turning into Athol Street after an afternoon spent begging the butcher for the cheapest scraps of meat and the fruit and veg hawker for his last remaining apples for pennies, I bumped straight into Lizzy, almost dropping my basket.

'Oi watch what yer doin'! Oh our Maggie, didn't see it was yous. Don't mind me, don't know where me manners have gone.' Lizzy smiled her lovely smile, and brushed her sleeve down where we'd collided.

'I was on me way to see ye, got somethin' to tell you that I know yer'll want to hear, queen.'

Lizzy linked her arm into mine and I gave her a questioning look. 'What is it, our Lizzy. I haven't got time fer games today,' I frowned.

I was shattered. I'd spent most of the afternoon hauling water from the pump and onto the range to set to boil so that my siblings could have their weekly scrub down. It had been hard graft, and now I was desperate for a soak myself before Da got home.

'All right, queen, I won't muck you around. Them's looking for girls fer the factory floor, and I told them you'd do!'

'What are ye goin' on about, our Lizzy. I can't work, I've got enough on me hands without eight hour shifts at the ice cream factory—' I started to reply.

'It's decent wages, and we all get on, like. Every Friday night there's a dance we all go to, proper good fun. Nice fellas there as well.' Lizzy gave me a conspiratorial wink and nudged my shoulder as I laughed my response.

'Me dad'll never let me go to work now. There's too much to be done at home, though a few extra shillings in the pot each week wouldn't go amiss, I'll give ye that,' I conceded, suddenly thrilled at the mere possibility of getting a proper job.

'Go 'ed, I thought I'd talk ye round, now be off with ye and tell yer da that it's time you went out into the world and earned yerself a few pennies!' Lizzy cackled as she sped off.

It must've been her day off as I'd rarely seen her since she started work at the factory. When I did see her, she'd always be full of it, the dances, the good times and laughs the factory girls were all having. The jealousy I had been suppressing rose up in me and I felt sick to my stomach.

All ye can do, girl, is ask, I said to myself as I walked the last few yards back to our dingy rooms.

Later that evening, after Da had his long soak in the bath, and eaten the dinner I'd prepared for us all, I braced myself to ask the question I'd wanted to ask since the day I walked out of school. He was sitting by the fire in his usual place, his hair wet from his soaking and a small smile on his lips. His solid, humble face was creased into the premature lines that hard work gave the people round our way. He looked older than his fifty-one years, and suddenly I felt a thrill of fear. He was so much the cause of our safety and security that I could hardly bear to think he was a mortal man like any other. Without him, we'd be sunk.

'Ye look like yer've seen a ghost, our Maggie,' Da looked over at me, watching my mouth intently for my response.

I couldn't speak. My throat had clenched tight and I couldn't find it within me to ask him if I could go and get work. I knew it was up to me to take care of him, and if that meant sacrificing a job and an exciting new social life at the factory then so be it. I shook my head, then bent it down to continue repairing the holes in Father's working jacket. A single tear dropped onto the rough fabric, sinking into the frayed sleeves.

When I told Lizzy later she reacted with frustration, but I knew she understood. Instead, she told me that if I couldn't work with the girls, I could come out and play with them instead.

'Play with them?' I queried.

'You know, come out with us and have a laugh. We're all goin' down the Scottie Road market tomorra to get ourselves a dress fer the dance the same night. So tell yer arl man yer comin', no arguments!'

It was settled. On Friday, after I'd discharged my duties, I raced down to meet Lizzy at the end of Athol Street. She was standing with two other girls who introduced themselves as Flora and Mary. Flora was a slim girl, perhaps a year or two older than Lizzy and me, with brown curly hair and a wicked gleam in her eye. Mary was the quieter of the two. She had the red hair of the Irish settlers and freckles, despite the lack of sunlight leaching into our squalid streets. She was plump and homely looking, and next to them both, Lizzy looked a radiant beauty, despite the fact they were dolled up to the nines wearing high-heeled shoes and red lipstick! All three girls had their hair rolled up in metal curlers in preparation for the dance.

'Yer'll have to set yer curls in pipe cleaners an' rags, our Maggie, if yer to look yer best fer tonight,' Lizzy nudged my arm.

I felt a little out of my depth but I made a mental note to do something about my shoulder length brown hair as I didn't want to be the drab of the group.

At that moment one of our local priests walked by, his black robes in stark contrast to the fluttering, bright beauty of the girls. In unison we all muttered a sober 'Hello Father' before peeping up from our downcast eyes to judge when the coast was clear of spiritual direction. We linked arms, and chattering at ten to the dozen, we hollered 'All right, queen' to people we knew, dodging the occasional motor car that swept past us on the cobbled street and chuckling with the delight of a free afternoon to spend rummaging through the stalls of 'Paddy's Market', which was our nickname for it.

Da had been thrilled when I said I was going. He'd slipped me three shillings from his 'savin's' – kept in a jam jar under the head end of the iron bed, heaven knows how he'd managed to save them but he had. And I felt like real royalty with the weight of the coins in my purse, heading down to the bustling market to look for a second-hand frock.

I wrapped my wool shawl round my shoulders, the days

still had a nip of frost in the air. The market was a flavour of the exotic shores that lay way beyond our reach, beyond the lurching Irish Sea and perilous waters of the Mersey River. Among the crowds of locals were men with saffron-coloured skin, some even with skin as dark as the coal tar we foraged for our fires. We called them all 'coolies' and gawped at these men from India, Asia and Africa who had found a home among our teaming dockland streets. We knew no better, and we delighted in the strange sights, the cheap scents and scarves they were selling.

One man had a stack of hats on his head that he seemed to pile up and walk about with ease. We delved into heaps of clothes, most of which I guess had been thrown away by people better off than we'd likely ever be. I didn't stop to worry. I'd seen a periwinkle blue dress that looked like it would fit. Holding it up to my body, I looked quizzically at the girls.

'What d'ye think?' I said, looking down at the cotton frock.

'Ar'ey what's she like?!' chanted Mary and Flora together, before collapsing into giggles.

'Ye look like the bees knees, girl, yer'd better buy it before ye change yer mind,' prompted Lizzy.

Even before I'd handed over the coins I felt guilty about spending so much of our family's money. It didn't seem right, me having a treat when the others were having bread and dripping for tea. I looked down at the dress again. It did look like it was made for me, the exact same colour as my eyes and with an A-line skirt that flared out from my waist.

Without thinking any more, I handed over the money, feeling breathless with excitement. I was going to my first dance this evening, and I had the perfect dress to wear.

Now all I had to do was run home, set the pot to boil, get the dinner done and race out again to meet the factory girls and get the bus to the dance hall. I made my apologies and left, agreeing to meet them at the same spot a few hours later.

No matter how hard I tried I couldn't get my hair to form a single curl, as was the fashion, so instead I had to settle for brushing it smooth and enjoying the feel of my new clothing next to my skin. Entering the kitchen, Da turned to pour hot water into his tea cup, but seeing me he stopped, put down the enamel kettle, and wiped his forehead. In that moment I was aware that something had changed. Perhaps in his eyes I was no longer his 'little girl', I was growing into a woman. He smiled that warm, familiar smile and nodded.

'Yer look a beauty, our Maggie, a real beauty,' was all he said. His voice sounded choked, his throat constricted with emotion.

Suddenly shy, I peeped back at him, aware that however restricted my life was, there were still some things that changed, and my transition to womanhood was one of them. I blew him a kiss, grateful for his love.

'Go 'ed, look at the time, I'm late!' The realisation jolted me out of our reverie. Even though he couldn't hear me, I sang: 'I'm off out, Da, clattering down the steps and out into the court.

Well, they all looked a picture. With their hair curled and shiny, wearing new frocks and their high heels and stockings, I felt instantly dowdy in comparison.

'Come 'ere, our Maggie, let's do the finishin' touches,' said Lizzy, brandishing a red lipstick which she applied to my startled lips.

'Yer've got stockings on, where did ye get those?' I gawped, staring at Lizzy's tan-coloured slender legs with the telltale brown line running up the back of them.

'Those aren't stockin's ye daft cow, them's gravy browning and me mam's eyebrow pencil!' snorted my friend.

I looked back at them in amazement. Now she'd told me, I could see they were drawn on, but from a distance they looked like the real thing.

'Yer'll 'ave to show me how to do that, like,' I grinned, 'are we ready to get goin'?'

'Yer just need a touch of powder, that'll see yer right, then we're done,' finished Lizzy. Specks of powder caught the light from the gaslight above us as she applied it to my up-turned face. 'Ye look beautiful, our Maggie. What I wouldn't do to have those blue eyes of yours,' she said with her soft Irish lilt.

We smiled at each other under the low orange light.

'Yer'll do, now let's get a move on girls, or all the good'uns'll be gone!' laughed Flora, and together we clattered off to the bus stop.

The dance hall was packed. The boys stood awkwardly on one side of the room, while the girls fidgeted and gossiped on the other. Every now and then a brave lad would walk stiffly over to someone and ask them to dance. As the boy walked across the room, the girls swayed like flowers seeking the sunshine, leaning over to see who would be the lucky girl. I was just watching a pretty girl with strawberry blonde hair and pink cheeks get picked, when I heard a cough next to me. I swivelled round.

'May I 'ave this dance, like?' said Thomas McGee, my old childhood sweetheart!

Well, I hadn't seen much of Thomas since he'd left school

before me. I'd missed him, of course. As children we'd shared secrets and laughs, holding hands as we walked through our streets, Thomas stealing a peck on the cheek now and again. He used to bring me little gifts to share after school, like a soft rounded pebble from the dockside or a raven's wing. His gestures had been very naive, very childish, but sweet and carefree. By the time he left school, I'd had to grow up faster than perhaps was usual, and so his absence had not hit me as hard as it might otherwise have done. My life became too busy caring for my siblings and father, leaving me little time for innocent romance and companionship.

Thomas cleared his throat again and I realised he was nervous. I blinked and felt suddenly very anxious. I hadn't banked on being a girl that was asked to dance, and by someone who was at once so familiar yet a stranger to me. I'd seen Thomas now and again over the years, running through the tenements on errands, kicking a ball in the streets with other local lads, but I hadn't spoken to him since he'd become a full-grown man, and now I had the chance my mind had frozen.

I stammered 'yes' as he led me onto the dance floor, drinking in the sight of him. He looked well enough, in fact he cut rather a dashing figure with his dark hair and deep brown eyes, which I couldn't help noticing. We danced one dance, and then another.

He didn't say much. Thomas lived in one of the courts on Newsham Street, just off Scotland Road, and was now a man of seventeen. He was another whose ancestors had come over from Ireland during the Great Famine. We smiled shyly at each other then another lad cut in and I was whisked away on his arms. I stole a glance back at Thomas. He was standing on the edge of the dancers, looking straight at me. I felt a shiver down my spine. I pulled my gaze away and moved to the big band beat, with the satisfaction of knowing that he was watching every move I made.

CHAPTER 6

Wedding Bells

November 1937 – 30 September 1938

'I luv ye Maggie Riley, and I'm goin' to marry ye, yer'll see.'

My face reddened as Thomas McGee took my hand and looked at me with that serious expression of his. We had stopped walking as we were back at Latimer Buildings on Latimer Street, on the east side between Athol Street and Slade Street, where Da, Nellie, Tommy and I were now living. The unscrupulous landlord of our Athol Street flat had increased the rent beyond what Da could afford, and so we'd been left with little choice but to find somewhere else. The two rooms we shared were slightly better than our old ones round the corner, but still I wasn't hurrying back to get inside them despite the fact it was a chill November night in 1937.

I leaned back against the black brick of the building. As Thomas breathed, the air became swirls of vapour, which settled around us. Peeping at him from under my lashes, I took in Thomas's handsome face, his strong athletic frame, his dark hair and moustache. Just then he leaned in for an embrace, but I was a good Catholic girl and I wasn't going to be the butt of the local gossips so I pushed him away, smiling.

'Go 'ed, our Thomas, I'm not goin' to kiss ye here like a floozy!' I laughed, but quick as a weasel, Thomas grabbed my waist and snatched a kiss from me anyway.

'Hey!' I said, indignantly, fighting him off, 'don't ye go

tryin' to smooch me, Thomas McGee, what'll people say?'
The moonlight spared my blushes, but I wasn't letting him
get away with that.

'I don't care what people say, Maggie. I told yer just now
I'm goin' to marry ye and so if I want a kiss I shall have one.'
He cocked one eyebrow as he replied.

I tutted my response, then flicked my skirts round and
threw a goodbye over my shoulder. It was too cold to stand
around being flirted with by Thomas McGee, even though
we'd had a nice evening at the Rotunda Theatre together. If I
didn't hurry back home, I'd get 'what-for' from Da for being
out late, because he always, always stayed up to see me come
in, bless him.

Thomas and I had been courting for a few months now,
and tonight he'd taken me out, but it was the first time
he'd mentioned marriage. I didn't think much of it. I have
never been a sentimental person, I've always been one to get
on with things, I didn't waste time on romance stories, or
mushy love stuff. Besides, I'd been born and raised a Catholic, and had always stuck to the values of those traditions,
both morally and spiritually. But I have to admit that I liked
the look of him, and we both seemed to enjoy each other's
company. Whether my knees went weak at the sight of him,
well, that was something I'd never admit to in a million
Sundays!

I was proud to be courting him, though. I knew that all the
girls in our street were jealous of me. Thomas was known as
the local 'catch' with his dark good looks, and I was proud
as punch to be known as his sweetheart. We'd met again
two-and-a-half years ago at the dance, but it had taken him
till two months ago to pluck up the courage to ask me out
formally. On our first date he'd taken me to the pictures to
see the film reels, and it was there I was kissed for the first

time at the age of seventeen. I'll admit to a small fluttering of my heart, but as I said, I'm not one for romance, I had too much to do and too many chores to harbour any illusions like that.

As I pushed through the door into the main living space that had a curtain strung across it to create a bedroom for Nellie and me, I saw my father dozing in his chair by the still glowing embers of the fire. His face looked peaceful and still and so I tiptoed across the room, trying not to wake him. I poured myself a cup of water and gulped it down, putting the cup on the side without making a sound. Even so, Da snuffled then coughed, blinking his eyes open and looking round the room for the source of his sleepy confusion.

'It's only me, Da. Just helpin' meself to a drink. Why don't ye get to bed now, ye must be dead beat,' I said softly, hearing Nellie's gentle sighs as she slept behind the sagging fabric of the curtain.

I helped my father, who was a strong man of fifty-three and still worked twelve- or even eighteen-hour shifts at the dockside daily. The foremen at the dock gates all took pity on him as he was deaf and injured, so they gave him work, knowing he had us to feed and clothe by himself. It was how we looked after each other, but with the knowledge that if Da was given work there were plenty who weren't. Still, he needed his sleep.

After I'd pulled his scratchy wool blanket over him I took off my shoes and coat and placed them carefully in the living room that was also our kitchen and shared bedroom. Nellie was fast asleep, her arm flung over the side of the iron bed, the covers draping onto the floor. I tucked her back in, even though she was a big girl of nine years old, then wiggled into the bed, doing my best not to disturb her. She rolled over at one point, making a gurgling sound in her throat, but soon settled back into her dreams. I lay there, staring up at the filthy ceiling of the rat-infested hovel we had nicknamed 'the garret', and wondered if Thomas meant what he said, whether he really intended on marrying me.

'Stop there, our Maggie, and turn to me. Don't she look beautiful. Jaysus, yer a sight for sore old eyes,' laughed Mrs Jones from Athol Street. Our beloved former neighbour was fixing the white ribbon to my hair, draping it down one side, framing my face in a style similar to the decade just passed.

'Ye look like an angel,' said Nellie in her girlish voice, despite the fact she was now a bonny young girl of ten years old. Nellie was wearing her Sunday best dress, an off-white smock that showed off her blossoming beauty perfectly. I was standing by the window of the main room we shared. Apart from the curtain and the iron bed, there was little else in the room; our wooden kitchen table, the three rickety chairs, a rug and all the bits I needed to perform my chores: the brush, a bucket and several scrubbing brushes. The table was usually bare, or covered in crumbs from Nellie and Tommy's mealtimes, but today it was festooned by flowers, or so it looked to me. In reality there was only a small posy for me to hold in church, and a buttonhole each for Da and Tommy.

It was 9 February 1938, and it was my wedding day. Thomas had been as good as his word.

'Stand still, our Maggie, and ye can take that look off yer face!' chortled Mrs Jones. She finished fiddling with my bow and stood back, her lumpen body masking the small light through the window. 'Ye look grand, a proper lady, like,' she declared, and we all laughed.

I had been grimacing where she'd pulled the ribbon too tight, but all I could feel now was the warmth of her love, and the excitement that today I would become Thomas McGee's wife. I looked down at the white dress I was wearing. Instinctively, I held my hand over my slim stomach, that wasn't yet showing signs of the new life growing inside me.

In spite of all I'd said and thought about my faith, in spite of my values, in spite of everything that made me, me, I'd succumbed to Thomas's charms and we'd made love. I know I should've regretted it. After all, there wasn't much worse you could do in our community. Perhaps I wanted the love he offered me, or perhaps I wanted to be transported away from the menial chores and my domestic life for just a few precious moments. I don't know why I compromised myself and my faith, but I didn't regret it, just as I didn't regret the life that was growing inside me, God strike me down.

I had been terrified when I realised that the sickness I experienced every morning that had me running out to the shared lavvy was the first sign of my pregnancy. I'd confided in my beloved Mrs Jones and she'd cackled when she saw my white face and felt my stomach, which had already just started to protrude. Then, when she saw my horror and my tears, she swept me into her arms and rocked me like a baby.

'Don't ye fret, our Maggie,' she'd crooned. 'Yer Thomas'll do right by ye or he'll have me and yer da to face. It'll all be all right. Ye aren't the first girl around these parts to fall in the family way, and Thomas is a good-looking one all right. I reckon Our Lady herself'd have a job to resist him!'

The hardest thing though was telling Da. In a profound way, I felt I'd let him down. I waited one evening till after he'd finished his dinner. I didn't hesitate. I blurted out my news as soon as Tommy and Nellie were in bed, making sure Da's eyes were fixed on my lips as I spoke.

He was silent for a long while, then he turned to me with a beaming smile on his face. In that moment, I knew that whatever had happened me and my baby would be OK. Da was happy to have a grandchild! He was surely the kindest, most loving man in the world. I hugged him tightly, feeling his strength and warmth against me, sending a quiet prayer of intense gratitude to the Virgin Mary for the blessings in my life, determined this baby would be one of them. When I broke the news to Thomas, he immediately said we had to wed straight away. There were many girls who weren't so lucky, and who never got that precious ring on their finger, so I was relieved and happy to marry Thomas. And yet, when I'd told him, I sensed something in him change. It was nothing I could yet verbalise, but I felt a coldness creep in to his manner, so different from my own father's response.

Despite that, our wedding day dawned on 9 February 1938, and I felt grateful that our child, conceived in love, would be born in wedlock. I fitted into the dress that I'd borrowed from another of my neighbours, Rita, a lovely girl who'd been made up for me when I told her I was getting married.

'Ye must borrow me dress,' she'd said, 'I won't take no fer an answer. It bought me good luck I'll say,' she laughed and patted her proud, round stomach, full with the latest child she carried.

I had slipped the dress on, wishing my mam could have seen this day, despite everything she'd put us all through. Obviously I didn't miss her drinking and her tempers, but I still carried the notion that we weren't a 'proper' family without her, however much Da loved us and looked after us. It was a stupid thought, but even so, a girl without her mother on her wedding day seemed a sad thing.

'Ready, girl?' asked Da softly.

I often wondered if he picked up on my thoughts, guessing how much I missed having my mother around. He was so gentle, so kind. I couldn't have wished for a better father, but I still felt there was something missing that day, which I guess there was. I smiled to him, swamped by my love for him, and nodded, linking my arm through his.

He'd pawned back his Sunday suit to wear to take me down the aisle at St Sylvester's Church in Silvester Street. We weren't far from the church we worshipped in, and so we set off on foot, walking to the ceremony, a small band of God-fearing people, walking the streets we were rooted within.

Outside the front gate of the red-brick tower of St Sylvester's I hesitated. This was the moment I'd waited for, dreamed about. The bell tower seemed to reach far into the blue sky above me and I felt small and deliciously insignificant next to God's universe.

'I'm ready,' I whispered, stepping forwards towards the ritual that would bind Thomas and me together in the eyes of God.

My heart banged in my chest as I stood in front of the priest, resplendent in gold and white robes. I sneaked a look at Thomas standing next to me, staring ahead, intent on the priest's opening prayer.

'Father, ye have made the bond of marriage a holy mystery, a symbol of Christ's love fer his Church . . .' the priest's voice undulated, filling the mostly empty church. We were only few, just family, to witness our special day. I willed Thomas to look at me, to acknowledge me and reassure me it was just us getting married, just me and Thomas making a life together. He carried on staring ahead, a slight frown on his handsome silhouette. I gave myself up to the service, letting the words from the Gospel wash through me in this most holy of sacraments.

When it came to the exchange of the rings, Thomas looked down as he placed the ring on the finger of my left hand. It slid into place as if it had always been there. I did the same to Thomas, hoping he'd meet my eyes as I spoke, 'Thomas McGee, take this ring as a sign of my love and fidelity.' The church was hushed. The priest's voice rang out with the Prayers of the Faithful. I murmured, 'Lord hear our prayer,' looking down at the small gold band on my finger. Thomas earned good money in the army and had been granted special leave for our wedding day.

He looked so smart, dressed in his full military uniform, his moustache neat and groomed. As we posed for our photograph after the ceremony, I felt serene, blessed by God and sealed into our union. I fervently hoped Thomas felt the same, though he spoke little that day.

The rest of the occasion passed in a blur. There were a few drinks shouted by my father in a nearby alehouse, but there was no money for a party or dinner so we did the best we could, and by the evening I was back in my usual outfit having returned the wedding dress to my new friend. Then Thomas and I headed out to the pictures to see the film reels.

I barely paid attention, so excited was I to finally be Thomas's wife. I twisted my ring, checking it was still there, still real, and kept looking sideways at my new husband as he watched the flickering screen. We knew we only had this night together.

Thomas was posted back to India the next morning, and if things went the way the reels predicted then goodness knows what awaited our country in the years ahead. We all hoped for peace, but the rise of the Nazi Party in Germany made us all nervous. There was talk of war – and we all hoped that's all it would be: talk. Surely there couldn't be another, after the one that should've ended all wars? It could hardly be imagined, and yet that feared word kept cropping up. The whispers were that we were heading that way, and no one or nothing was going to stop it.

Creeping back into the garret, Thomas dropped his hat on the bed, his face was dark in the shadows. We were wed now. Our union was sanctified by God and we could at last be together as man and wife. Yet, Thomas didn't seem himself.

Perhaps he's worried about going back to the army tomorrow? I thought to myself, biting my lip. I had a nagging thought that maybe Thomas regretted marrying me, but I knew I was also tired and overwrought. The day had brought up mixed emotions, a sense of safety and security at being wed, but also the loss of my mother, which I hadn't expected to feel so acutely once more.

Tommy and Nellie were bedded down in the only bedroom, while Da slept in his usual place by the fire. We'd made sure we stayed out as late as possible, knowing how awkward it would be to spend our first night together as a lawfully wed couple in such intimate surroundings. Somehow we managed to get into the creaking, sagging bed with its thin mattress and wool blanket without disturbing my father. The wall was crawling with lice and cockroaches, which froze as soon as we lit a candle stub.

'Pesky bloody creatures,' I swore.

'Mary, Mother of Jaysus, that's the first time I've heard a swear word coming out of yer mouth, Maggie,' was all Thomas said.

I felt suddenly shy. I placed a hand protectively across the small bump that was only just starting to show. I'd looked forward to our wedding day but it felt different from how I'd imagined it. Later that night, I watched as Thomas lay asleep, I saw his breath enter and leave him by the thin light of the city moon. He looked so peaceful, so young, even though he was twenty-one now. Again, I felt a shiver, a sigh of the disquiet I couldn't shake off. When would I see him again? Such a simple question, and one that no man on earth could answer.

When the cold dawn light finally woke him, Thomas rubbed his eyes and stretched, yawning into the morning. I'd barely slept and my head felt fuzzy, disorientated. Here I was, a married woman, about to say goodbye for God knew how long, to my new husband.

He dressed swiftly. I offered to make him tea but he shook his head. 'I have to go,' he said, simply, buckling his leather belt and pulling on his army boots.

Thomas stood above me. I sat hunched on the bed, drawing my legs in, feeling like I was out of my depth and I wasn't sure why. He did up his shirt buttons, pulled on his jacket and turned to me, a shadow falling across his face. He didn't say a word but leaned over and kissed me full on the lips.

'Thomas . . .' I stammered, not knowing what I wanted to say, but he had his hand on the door knob and had eased it open, quietly so as not to wake the others.

He made the gesture to shush me, one finger over his mouth, like you would make to a small child, and he left, walked out, his boots echoing on the steps, fading away into the morning. That was it. He was gone.

I suddenly felt a sense of loss that overwhelmed me. The father of the child that grew within me, now my husband, had walked out without a backwards glance. He was walking into unsettled times, and he left me with no idea of when he might return. The room suddenly felt empty, and I think in that moment my heart broke for the second time. His kisses and embraces had seemed cold, less emotional than our earlier days of courting. His manner was stiff. The gentleness, the words of love, had been replaced with a kind of formality that I didn't understand.

I realised that Thomas had been itching to get away. Perhaps he felt he had done the right thing now and was free to go? He had always talked about wanting to see the world, his dreams of travel with the army. Perhaps the reality of married life paled compared to the excitement of new sights and sounds in India? I didn't know. We hadn't had time to talk. We'd been married less than twenty-four hours but already he felt like he was a world away from me.

I felt as alone as I'd ever felt in my life. I gathered in my body around me, as if protecting myself from any further emotional blows. Tears rolled down my face, wetting my cheeks and my knees. Thomas would be walking through the cobbled streets, each step taking him further from me and our child. I had no idea when he'd be home again. I had no idea even if he loved me any more.

His departure felt cold-hearted, but perhaps it was my tiredness and grief at seeing Thomas leave that haunted me, I started to tell myself. Perhaps there was nothing wrong and I merely had to adjust to new circumstances, as I'd done so many times before. I pushed my hair back from my face and the sheen from the gold ring winked at me. I had to carry on as if everything was OK. I had to keep calm and steady, and hope that Thomas and I could build ourselves a future with our child. Life had to carry on, and I had a baby to think about now.

Sighing, I eased off the sagging bed, aching as if I'd spent a night working at the docks like Da.

No time fer worryin', girl, get them pots to boil and water in the kettle, I told myself, pulling on my dress and apron, making ready for another day where nothing had changed, and yet everything had.

Spring became summer, and as August arrived I knew that soon my child would be here, too. Somehow I had managed to carry on with my chores throughout my pregnancy, though Da was always urging me to 'tek it easy, girl', though I worried about how I'd cope once the baby arrived. It didn't help that since Thomas had left, I had received nothing by way of correspondence from him. Nothing. No letters, nor cards, nor even the formalities associated with the death of a soldier abroad. Nothing. At first I'd assumed he was working too hard to write. Then, as the weeks passed, I started to worry.

I woke in the middle of the night when my labour pains started. Unusually, perhaps, given what I'd been told to expect, my fear of the contractions faded as they surged through my body. As I began the arduous journey into motherhood, my worries suddenly diminished. I had longed for this day, longed for the sensation of cradling Thomas's and my baby in my arms, and I suddenly felt like a woman, a mother, who would cope with whatever followed as long as I protected my baby and fought for her safety and well-being.

Nellie roused Da and between them they got me to Walton Hospital, where seven hours later I held my daughter. I kissed her soft downy head and wept both with the joy of meeting her, and the sorrow of knowing Thomas had missed this moment. Nellie and Da had stayed with me at the hospital overnight until they could hold Rita, the newest member of the McGee family, in their arms.

Da wiped away a few tears, looking grey and old in the morning light, before leaving to start his twelve-hour shift at the dockside. Nellie went home to get Tommy's breakfast, leaving me holding my child, feeling like a full grown women at last, though I was only eighteen years old.

Rita was baptised only a few days later, at St Sylvester's Church. It was a special day, surrounded by a few friends and my family, yet sadness hovered at the edge of the ceremony, the absence of her father felt so complete, so final, that I felt very alone as I stood at the font and listened to the priest intone the familiar, sacred words. I hid my sadness as best I could from those around me so I didn't worry them needlessly, but Da knew, he could sense things. That night he drew me into his silent embrace where, for a moment, I felt the safety and love I had from him as a child. Gazing at my sleeping daughter later that night, I vowed that I would stop my fretting about her father and concentrate on making her the happiest little girl in Latimer Street.

More than a month later, on 30 September 1938, I was ladling hot scouse into my brother Tommy's proffered plate at dinner when Da cleared his throat. We all looked up from our soft chatter in astonishment. Our father was a man of few words, yet here he was about to make a speech that I would remember for the rest of my days: 'They say at the pen that we're going to war, that it's really goin' to happen.'

I started to interrupt, after all today was the day that Neville Chamberlain had signed the Munich Agreement, to appease Hitler and his German armies, but Father held up his hand to stop me. I sat down, shocked into silence, and cradled Rita to my breast. This sounded serious.

'The dockers say we're goin' to war so we'd better be

ready. If those German bastards bomb us like they say they will, then we'll be a target.'

I touched Da's hand lightly, to show him I needed to speak. He turned his head to look at my face, to understand me in his silent world.

'But it's peace now, everyone says so, and even if it isn't we'll be safe here won't we, like? Those Germans'll bomb London not us, won't they? Surely we don't have to worry? After all, what was the point of all that appeasement and signing papers?' Suddenly the world seemed a frightening, and confusing place again.

My brother Tommy was almost a man, almost sixteen. He'd left school more than a year ago and started work as a firefighter, and we were all so proud of him. He was a gentle boy, shy and self- contained, the image of his father. Nellie, who was ten years old, and a sweet girl, was staring at Father, her mouth open in a mixture of disbelief and something else, an understanding of sorts that life might be about to change and we were powerless in the face of the strong currents sweeping our nation.

'I don't want to scare ye all,' continued our father, seeing our shock, 'but forearmed is forewarned. The dockers say the appeasement means nothing, that Hitler'll stop at nothing, and no paper's goin' to stop him, like. The docks'll be on Hitler's targets, if it ever comes to that, and only God knows how we'll manage.'

Da sat down, then Tommy's voice piped up. 'If those Jerry bastards come anywhere near us, I'll fight. I won't stand fer it, and neither will most of the lads around here.'

He looked fierce in that moment and I felt so proud of him, standing up for what was right. Despite that I felt a shiver down my spine, though the evening was mild for September.

Father had lip read Tommy's grand speech. 'Yer'll have no

choice, son, if they invade, like. We'll all 'ave to do our bit fer the war effort. But until then, let's eat our dinner and enjoy bein' together.'

Da bent his head and held his hands together in the age-old gesture of supplication. We said grace and ate our meal in silence, with only the sounds of our slow, thoughtful chewing. Perhaps war was really coming, and if it was, we'd better get used to the idea.

CHAPTER 7

Letters to Thomas

Autumn 1939 – January 1940

'Hello me little darlin', yer mam's beautiful babby, so you are . . .' I smiled into the bonny pink face of my daughter Rita, as I held out my arms to her.

'Come to yer mam, come on now,' I cooed again, watching as her plump fists let go of the chair leg. Like a colt reared from its mother, she put one wobbly foot in front of the other. 'That's it, girl, ye keep comin' to Mam.'

My voice was deliberately calm so that I didn't disturb her first, momentous steps across the small kitchen and living area. She almost caught her foot in the single rug spreading out from under the wooden table but she stayed upright, chuckling with the newness of her independence and holding her plump little arms aloft. Slowly my baby girl tottered towards me, a huge toothless grin spreading across her pink face. All at once she fell into my open arms, in a warm bundle of giggles.

'Yer such a big girl now, our Rita, where did me wee babby go?' I laughed with mock surprise, incredulous at how the months had gone by so quickly, adding softly, 'Yer dadda would be so proud of ye, walkin' like a grown-up girl, he'll be so sorry he missed it, so sorry.'

I paused, feeling the empty space between my ribcage where my happiness should've been. Instead, my heart ached with a loneliness that I sometimes felt would swallow me whole. And the cause of it? Well, I hadn't heard a word from my Thomas since he'd left for India the day after he married me. Our wedding night was the only night we'd spent together as man and wife. I knew that he'd be busy, but to have heard nothing from him, well it wasn't right, was it?

I had a single photograph of us, taken on our wedding day. Thomas looked so handsome, standing tall next to me. How many times had I gazed down at his angular face, at his sweep of black hair and black military moustache, wondering why on earth he'd forgotten us so quickly. I was still as taken with his dark good looks as the day I'd become his wife. In that sepia-stained photograph that I kept by my bedside, I was wearing my white dress with a white ribbon in my hair. We looked so young, so proud to be married. I just couldn't fathom why I'd heard nothing since the morning after.

He'd dressed himself in his uniform, given me a kiss then walked out of our garret door. Sitting hunched on the bed, separated from Father by the thin curtain that divided the room, I hugged my knees and prayed it wouldn't be long before I saw him again because they were uncertain times. When he was posted away in February 1938 there was trouble on the horizon, or so the papers had said, and they were right, of course. I'd had a new life growing in my belly. A mere fluttering of a presence inside me. Enough life already in there to give me a mother's fierce love, fierce protectiveness.

As the weeks and months went by, my tummy swelled as my heart slowly contracted. *Are ye dead, Thomas?* My whispered pleas were lost in the fog and stench of the docklands summer months as we all stewed in the rancid mess of people, animals and industry. But still I waited, hoped and prayed. I'd written to him, of course I had. Every day at first. My early letters were filled with stories about our lives here, my growing belly, the wait for our child to be born. In one letter sent only three months after he left for India, I'd simply written:

Thomas, Husband, It feels strange calling you that as we've had only one night together as husband and wife. I haven't heard from you. Have you written? I guess you must have and somehow it's got lost. You are so far away in India. I wonder what that must be like? Our baby grows bigger every day, my stomach is so rounded I feel as big as the moon. I wonder if you'll recognise me when you come home. I don't know what to say. It's even stranger to write to someone I haven't spoken to for months so I'll just say, come home soon. Everyone says there's going to be a war. I hope you are safe. Please write to me soon. Your loving wife, Maggie

Then, as the weeks went by and I heard nothing from him, my letters dropped to once every two or three days, and now I put pen to paper once a week. I insisted on writing, I had to let him know we missed him and were hungry for news from him, yet the silence distressed and unnerved me. War had broken out, as Da had predicted it would, on 3 September of this year. Even with this momentous change, I had not received a single word from Thomas, even to reassure me that this phoney war, as it had been called, posed no threat to him. He was out there somewhere, yet he didn't write; he didn't write to me.

Thomas had known I was pregnant, and of course it spurred us into our marriage, I'm ashamed to say it. But he did the right thing by Rita and me. He made me respectable so I could hold my face up at Mass every Sunday without the dreadful sniggers and gossiping that those less fortunate girls who found themselves in the family way with no wedding ring on their finger had to endure. I'd avoided all that, and for that, at least, I was grateful to him.

The threat of imminent war had overshadowed our lives, skewed our values for the better, or so I thought. Where once our community would have condemned a couple marrying with a baby already in the belly, somehow when we faced the prospect of our menfolk, our husbands, brothers and fathers being blown to bits in foreign lands then perhaps we felt it wasn't worth adding to the possible heartache. Once the wash house gossip had been all 'What's she like? 'Avin' a babby with no sign of a ring on her finger ...' Now all that had gone. In a rush of steam and an uncertain future, we wondered when the fighting would start in earnest and whether the Germans really intended bombing us.

Our streets were close-knit, as only poor neighbourhoods could be. We'd always relied on the kindness of neighbours to see us through the hardest times, and if anything the threat of real warfare had brought us even closer. We all looked out for one another, while clicking the beads on our rosaries and praying for the phoney war to remain just that. And if a girl got herself in the family way, or even had to visit one of the women who 'helped girls out of trouble' then who were we to judge?

But Thomas had made it right and done the honourable thing. After all, he'd told me often enough he loved me and wanted me as his wife. We'd been childhood sweethearts, and I still remembered us pledging our love for each other when we were children, him pulling at my pigtails and whooping with happiness as we careered out of school together on many, many afternoons. The memories made his absence of contact even more distressing, and unfathomable.

Why don't yer write to me, our Thomas? I implored every day when I saw the postie climbing the steps to our flat. Each morning I opened the door, hoping, praying there'd be something for me. Each day he doffed his cap to me, and shook his head, handing over whatever post there might be for Da or a neighbour. No word. No letter. Again, silence. Despite this, I was determined to keep the faith and write to my man.

I tickled Rita again and she gurgled her delight. I set her down on the rug and she was quickly absorbed in playing with the old rag doll that used to be Nellie's. I watched her, delighting in the daughter that had been born from our union, and I decided to write again. My ink pen hovered over the thin cheap paper. How could I express the love I had for our daughter in mere words? How could I paint a picture of her, and how she looked today, clean from a wash in the tin bath, smelling of soap and talc? I inhaled the milky scent of her, looked again to see a slant of light catch her brown curls, and I began to write.

Several weeks after posting the letter, still having heard nothing back from my husband, I determined on another course of action. Gathering up Rita's little woollen jackets and bundling her into a swathe of blankets, I set off for London Road to the photographer's studio called Jerome's. I had been saving up spare pennies for months as I wanted to have some keepsake of Rita's baby years so that Thomas wouldn't miss out completely if he ever came home to us. I'd decided to get her picture taken. It hadn't occurred to me until now that I could post one out to him as a last-ditch attempt to prompt correspondence from him in any form.

I pulled a woollen beret onto my hair, looked at myself in the small cracked mirror and saw a woman staring back. A woman who had grown up years before her time, but who still had a fresh-faced look of optimism. I smiled at myself. I had survived until now, and would thrive again, no matter what happened, with or without Thomas in our lives, though it pained me even to think it.

It was a bright winter day, a day for optimism and ventures such as the one I was embarking on. At the studio, the receptionist made me wait for a few moments. She had blonde hair set in shiny rolls around her pudgy face, and bright red lipstick. She smiled at me as I jiggled Rita on my lap.

'She's an angel, Mrs McGee,' she said.

'Thank you, friend. She is,' I replied, feeling a fresh wave of motherly love wash over me.

'You can go through now, they're ready for you, Mrs McGee.' The woman pointed to a shabby door at the back of the shop. Even now the use of my married name sent a small lurch through my stomach. I was married in name only, and it felt sore, though I smiled brightly in response and wheeled Rita and her perambulator through to the back room. Tentatively pulling aside a black curtain that had seen better days, I found a blackened space with a large camera and a light.

'Just pop yer daughter down, and we'll see how she photographs,' said the kindly man behind the lens.

I knelt down with Rita and sat her on the sheepskin rug spread across the floor. My baby girl looked up at me as I backed off and burst into laughter, thinking this was some new game. 'Oh very good, very good. Excellent, yer'll be made up with these shots,' came the voice from behind the camera.

'Oh is that it?' I exclaimed, I wasn't sure what I'd expected but I was surprised it was done and dusted so quickly.

'All finished, she takes a lovely picture, Mrs McGee, a lovely picture, so if you'd kindly settle yer account at the front desk we'll send ye yer photographs once they're developed.'

Back at the two rooms we lived in, I sat nursing a lukewarm cup of tea while Rita had her afternoon nap on our small shared iron bed. My thoughts jumbled together; part sorrow, part excitement that Thomas might see his daughter at long last.

Once the images were done, and Father and I had pored over them choosing the best one of Rita, I posted it to Thomas. For the next few weeks, I waited with even more anticipation for the postman, but every day was the same. A small shake of the head as he delivered mail to the other rooms. Then a month after I'd sent out my missive, my plea to Thomas to find it in his heart to love his daughter, Da patted my shoulder and gestured for me to sit down at the kitchen table. He held my hand gently, like touching a newborn lamb, and I suddenly started to shake. I knew I wasn't going to like what he was going to say. I wanted to run away, overcome by a dread so deep I felt sucked under a strong current.

My father didn't waste his words. 'Look Maggie, he's either dead, or he's not worth the bother. You gorra forget about that Thomas right now, girl, or yer'll go mad with the waitin'.'

I looked into my father's tired face, creased into worry lines, and saw the anguish he'd been concealing from me. He felt things deeply did our da, and I saw that he'd known how much those pictures meant to me, and how badly I'd been hurt. I nodded, a tear sliding down my cheek, dropping onto my lap, blooming into a small stain on my apron. It was over, after 22 month lonely marriage of waiting and wishing. Whatever Thomas had meant to me, whatever feelings we once shared, it was gone. I had no answers, but I had to carry on and live my life, as hard as that might be.

I barely had time to grieve my lost love over the next couple of weeks. Christmas came and went with little festive cheer. The news that rationing would start had dampened already gloomy spirits. One cold morning in January 1940, Father,

Nellie and me were eating our dinner, some bacon ribs that I'd managed to procure from the butcher, when there was a knock at the door.

'Who could that be, like?' Da looked at me as if I knew. I shook my head.

Da got up and went to the door, opening it to find a policeman on the threshold of our home. 'Mr Thomas Riley, father of Thomas Riley?' the policeman said.

Da looked at me, not understanding due to his deafness.

I stood up. 'Yes, this is me father, Thomas Riley, and I have a brother Tommy, officer.' What else could I say? It wasn't every day the police turned up at our home! Just then I caught sight of Tommy standing behind the officer, looking down at his shoes, abashed. That wasn't like our Tommy, what could be going on?

'Officer, is there a problem, like?' I broke the awkward silence that had settled on the room.

'I'm sorry to have to tell ye but young Tommy Riley, here, was caught stealin' a pigeon out of a pigeon loft, and he'll have to go in front of the magistrate.' The man coughed, clearly feeling the tension that had suddenly filled the room.

'Caught stealin'!' Father stammered after I turned to him and explained, rather more loudly than the officer. My father was a very moral, a religious man. Stealing was anathema to him, as it was to all of us. Our Tommy was a good boy, he always had been. He was known for being reserved and gentle, like his da. To be in trouble with the law was so far from his usual character that we stood like fishes out of water, gawping between Tommy and the officer in complete shock.

The policeman cleared his throat again. 'Tomorrow morning, yer'll need to bring him down to the station and he'll go up before them.'

With that he looked at both of us to make sure we understood, then he touched the lip of his black helmet and turned to leave. I heard his heavy boots fade into the twilight, leaving us with Tommy and the shame that was written on his seventeen-year-old face.

I don't recall if Da said a word to Tommy that night. He was such a gentle man, I doubt he shouted his disapproval but my brother would have known, would've felt the disappointment emanating from his mild-mannered father.

The next morning both men, for Tommy was a man full grown, not a boy any longer, left the rooms, leaving me fretting and unable to settle on my chores until they returned. When they did, I took one look at Da's face and saw it was bad news.

'What is it? Our Tommy's not goin' to prison, is he? Oh Jaysus wept, not prison.' I couldn't help use a profanity, looking at Tommy's white-bleached face and seeing him clutch his cap in shaking hands.

'He's not goin' to prison, ye can set yer mind at rest, girl, but he's goin' to a bleedin' youth hostel in Wales for correction by the nuns up there,' said Father, 'and ye better get a move on and pack, our Tommy, as yer'll miss the bus otherwise.'

'A youth hostel in Wales?' I stammered. 'Fer how long?' was all I could think to say.

'For six months, a full six months.'

Well, I don't think I'd ever heard my father swear, even when Mam left.

'Six months! Our Tommy, what will we do without ye?' I wailed, running over to my 'little' brother and flinging my arms around him. I was as good as a mother to him, and I would miss him terribly. There was also the issue of the wage he brought into our home. What would we do without the money? We'd got used to those few extra coins in the kitty each week. We would struggle without them, that was for sure.

'But why did ye do it, Tommy?' I said out of sheer frustration, and not a little anger, when I'd wiped the tears from my eyes.

'I dunno, I just wanted me own pigeon. All the other fellas had one, and I thought old man Silas wouldn't miss one . . . I only wanted to borrow her, I'd have given it back, I swear it, our Maggie!'

In Tommy's voice I heard the yearning that only those brought up in real, desperate poverty can feel. He didn't steal it to be bad. He just wanted what he couldn't afford, and what he couldn't have. It was a similar story across our impoverished region, across the vast world that spanned the haves and the have-nots. A universal story of wanting something so very badly that the wanting becomes a part of your soul and you act in ways you never thought possible. Tommy was the most unlikely of thieves. He was a clean, well-brought-up boy with good manners and a gentle spirit, yet even he wasn't immune from the pull of taking something that wasn't his to own.

I couldn't blame him, and yet he'd done wrong, and he would have to go to Wales and stay in his hostel and pray with the nuns throughout the day as his own form of penance. This wasn't something that three Hail Marys and a few Our Fathers could rub out.

I sighed. 'Here, take the bread and drippin' sandwiches I made for dinner. I'll make some more when yer've gone, but I won't see ye starve on the journey.'

I wrapped up the mounds of roughly cut bread in a cloth, trailing crumbs across the table top, and handed them to him. He had little else to take, just his coat, his pyjamas and a spare vest.

I waved him off, wondering how he'd fare at Capel Curig camp in Betws-y-Coed. It sounded a million miles away. Wiping away yet more tears, I let Da and Tommy go, with more kisses and hugs for my brother.

Maggie, it might be the makin' of him, yer'll see, I reassured myself. The day seemed spent. I had to get used to putting out three plates each night not four, darning Da's socks and not Tommy's. I already felt the ache in my heart where my sweet brother resided, and I knew I'd miss him every second he'd be gone from us.

CHAPTER 8

Christmas Blitz

2–23 December 1940

A single snowflake danced through the white-grey sky. I held out my tongue to catch it, its icy softness dissolving, leaving behind a shiver of sensation. I huddled into my clothing, stamping my feet on the frozen cobbles, in an attempt to bring the life back to my chilled feet. All I had for warmth standing out at the two water taps in our bleak court was a woollen shawl wrapped tight around my threadbare dress. I stood in the queue, listening to the morning talk, the shared condolences. We hadn't had an air raid for several days, but the nightly threat of one, and the devastation left in each wake of the bombing's waves, was a real and present danger.

I would never forget the first time I heard the terrible wail of the siren, calling us into the shelters. It was the night of 28 August, only a few short months ago. I'd been ripped from my sleep by that deathly sound, and almost without thinking I grabbed Rita, shook Nellie and Da awake, then together we pulled on coats over pyjamas and thick nighties and hurled ourselves out into the court to join the scramble for the brick shelters that lined the streets.

There were few men racing to safety – most of our community's husbands and sons had signed up for active service, amid predictions that conscription would follow. Da's injuries excluded him from fighting and so we were blessed in having him with us. The terror of the crowds was palpable. Children sobbed, babies screamed, mothers hushed them and we all prayed with feverish intensity not to send those bombs near our babies. I clutched Rita to me tightly. Only Da looked serene. He couldn't hear a thing and sat rolling himself a ciggie with the calm of a stone-deaf man. I could have laughed out loud at the irony, except my throat was tight with fear and my eyes squeezed shut with the force of my prayers.

Liverpool had been second only to London in the pummelling it received from the German Luftwaffe. The drone of engines and the muffled eruptions as bombs hit their targets had become a familiar backdrop to our lives, with north Liverpool and the docks receiving the hardest blows. Only days earlier Queens Dock had been hit, becoming a furnace of raging orange fire, flames reaching into the dark night sky, the thick, black smoke of hell sitting over our city. And it wasn't just the docklands and its warehouses, railways and factories that bore the brunt of the enemy's raids. On that same night of 28 November, an air raid shelter at Durning Road containing 300 mothers, babies, children and those too old, injured or ill to sign up was hit. A parachute landmine smashed into the heart of the building, toppling the reinforced ceiling of the boiler room and killing 166 people in one swift, deadly strike. The grief was terrible. People clawed at the wreckage of twisted metal and shattered wood, at the piles of rubble and dust so thick it choked your lungs and blinded the rescue crews. It was a theatre of hell. A carnage so complete it stole the heart from our community, or so I was told. People, perhaps injured themselves, were desperate to find loved ones amid that flaming, burning burial ground. There were stories of people searching for the bodies of their families in the temporary morgues set up to house the dead, and finding only a piece of jewellery, a watch perhaps, that was the only way they could identify incinerated remains. Every night I would hear the stories, the grief-ridden tales of the carnage, and wonder to myself, was Mam in there? Had she perished? And, would I ever know if she had?

Churchill, who had become prime minister after Neville Chamberlain's resignation on 10 May 1940, called the Durning Road bombing the 'single worst civilian incident of the war', and he was right. And it happened in our city, our proud, shredded, battered city. Grief piled upon grief, loss and horror amid a sea of prayers from all faiths. I found comfort in church, but no answers. God's will was unfathomable to me, to us, but we accepted it and we worked with it as best we could.

Nothing I could do would stop the raids so I had to take my fears, my pleading, to my God, and hope He was listening.

The bombing had ceased after that night, but we knew to expect more and so carried on with life in the meantime. And now Christmas was fast approaching. It felt like the first real wartime Christmas, even though it was the second since war began, now that heavy rationing was in place, along with the bombing raids that had started over Liverpool in August. Despite the gloom and the fear, Nellie and I had made paper chains and festooned our drab rooms, bringing a small glimmer of the festive season into our lives. We had to keep our spirits up as the hardships bit, and the daily news of deaths both at sea, sky and on land flayed our souls.

Several women, clutching their tatty, frayed wool shawls round them, acknowledged me, nodding their heads, or saying 'all right, queen', frozen plumes from their mouths making ghostly shapes in the small court. The chill was bone-deep. It never left us from morning till nightfall, from waking to reaching into our deepest slumbers. We queued for water outside, boiled up kettles, lit our ranges and swept our floors with hands red raw with cold and hard work. My nails were bitten down, my back sore from hauling water and wet clothes, bending down to clean, scrub, lift and polish. As we stood stamping our feet on the cobbles, there was little of the gossip and laughter that had characterised our morning ablutions in the past. We each of us stood over the drain that cut the cobbled court in two, waiting for our turn to collect cold water into our kettles and buckets for the morning's tea and porridge, muttering and sighing with our burdens and losses.

When my time came, I slicked the freezing cold water across my face and hands, rubbing at the soot marks and dirt with a rag, breathing life back into my cold fingers. I filled the kettle, I couldn't bear to stay outside any longer and fill the bucket, and so would return later for water for the cleaning and the pot.

One of my neighbours, an elderly widow called Doris from across the street who lived with her daughter's family, beckoned me over to her. 'All right, our Maggie, did yer hear about Bill Armstrong and his wife Maggie?'

I walked over to the woman, bent low with her infirmities, and yet with clear, sharp eyes that belied her age. She wore a long black dress with the ubiquitous apron slung across her. It was filthy, and her front teeth were blackened and rotten, though she always seemed happy to talk and share the news of the day. Careful not to spill a drop of the water I'd collected, I wiped my brow as she spoke. 'Them and their five girls and babby boy died over at Rose Place, off Scottie Road. It happened the same night as the docks were hit. Terrible tragic it was. Me arl fella worked with Bill, and I'd met Maggie before. Friendly people, like.'

The old woman stopped and blinked up at me, checking I was listening. 'All of them gone with a single bomb, their home toppled like a stack of cards, like matchsticks. Makes yer think, don't it? None of us is safe, queen, not now those German bastards 'ave got our number.'

I let out a long, slow whistle. What could I say? In the face of such devastation, there was the sympathy I felt for those poor people, but if I'm honest, each new tragedy bought the relief, the gratitude, that it wasn't me or mine that were hurt or killed. I took those thoughts to my prayers each evening, asking God to take away my selfishness, yet the sly gratitude stayed with me. Nellie and Da were alive, my daughter, now two years old and growing into a lovely girl, was full of life and laughter despite the chaos surrounding her small life. Though the streets and houses of Liverpool contained piles of smoking wreckage and obliterated lives and buildings, that was proof positive of our luck so far.

Tommy had joined the Merchant Navy as soon as he returned from his exile to Wales in July. He'd spent his eighteenth birthday aboard a vessel on the Atlantic, becoming a man far from his family but doing important war work. A couple of weeks after his birthday, Da had received a letter, dated 24 October 1940, from Sister Monica, the Mother Superior of the youth centre where Tommy had been sent for his crime. In her slanting, elegant hand, she had written, asking how Tom fared at sea and expressing her fears for his safety:

A seaman's life is not an easy one in these days and they are doing a great work. I do hope he will have time to go to confession and Holy Communion.

I am sure any priest would help him do that. There are

*priests especially for seamen at Atlantic House, Fr Kelly and
Fr Waring. I wonder if Tom ever goes there.*

*We have all got to be ready these dreadful times, one is not
sure of their life for any length of time. I am sorry you have
been having such a rough time in dear old Liverpool recently.*

*We must place all our trust in God and keep praying.
Wishing you and your dear family every blessing. May our
dear Lord guard and protect you all.*

Da's voice became thick with emotion as he had read the missive out loud to us. Our Tommy. who was so beloved to us,
was blessed by those who cared for him through his troubled
times. It was a tribute to my brother's essential goodness, his
gentleness and good nature.

That evening Nellie and I had knelt for a long time in
front of the statue of Our Lady for our evening prayers, Rita
sleeping soundly in her cot. We prayed for our brother, and
for all those young men risking their lives on land or at sea. I
even prayed for my husband Thomas, wherever he was. Suddenly the war felt personal. It had taken our brother from us,
and all we could do was follow Sister Monica's advice and
pray for him as if our very lives depended on the strength of
those prayers.

Tommy was due to set sail again today, 2 December 1940,
after two weeks of home leave. Snow drifted from the gun-
metal grey skies and settled on our fractured city. I had said
many a goodbye to Tommy over the past few months with
each commission to go to sea, and here I was again, facing
the inevitable sadness at seeing my handsome brother leave
us again. He would be sailing on the *Arthur F. Corwin* tanker
from Gladstone Dock.

He loved the life at sea, the companionship, the shared

toils with crewmen. He'd always sworn that if there was war then he'd enlist as soon as he could. He, like so many others of our brave boys, had seen the pictures in the local papers of men queuing to fight for king and country, and vowed to do the same. We were so proud of him and all our fine young men. We watched them grow into manhood with a cheerful spirit, thinking this war must be over soon.

Tommy's latest work would be as a fireman aboard the tanker. Even though I should've been used to seeing Tommy go, something about this latest commission made me feel strangely vulnerable, a sense of fragility I couldn't explain. Because of this, I decided to travel with him on the tram to wave him off, leaving two-year-old Rita with Nellie. I'd never gone with him before; my life was too busy with chores. But that day I wanted to see him go myself, to witness a small part of the epic journeys he was undertaking, and to reassure myself that I'd shown him I cared in every possible way.

It was no surprise that Tommy had wanted to get aboard ship as soon as he was old enough. We Liverpudlians were outward-looking people, tied to the shifting waters of the river and the churning seas beyond for our livelihoods. Goods came and went. Exotic products, people, sights and smells passed through our neighbourhoods, never staying for long. Spices, grain and gum were bundled up and sent to the far reaches of Britain, and cargo sent out in return, the dockers loading and unloading against the backdrop of the quicksilver horizon. Yet now it was fighter planes from America that were delivered to our shores, war materials to be sent across the country, aircraft to be assembled at Speke Airport and shipped back out to the West African coast. Tommy had been chuffed to bits when he received his British Seaman's Identity Card after his initial five weeks of training, which he showed off to all who'd shown an interest. He'd reported to the Pool Office at the Liverpool waterside and been fingerprinted for the identity card. He was even able to boast that he earned an extra pound a week on top of his five-pounds-a-month salary as 'danger money', because the ship was transporting dangerous goods for the war effort, such as petrol and paraffin.

So Tommy and I jumped on the number 2 tram to Pier Head after eating our jam butty lunch in strange silence together, feeling the clack of the tramlines under our feet, swaying with the movement, and watching silently as our city swerved and rolled slowly past us. As we moved, my eyes swept the rubble and the still-smoking piles of brick, the twisted metal carcasses of buildings and factories. People stepped over the wreckage gingerly, carrying on with their business as if this was all completely normal.

We're resilient, us Scousers, I thought to myself, feeling a swell of pride towards my fellow citizens. The spectre of the last raids three days earlier haunted the city, a pall of grey hanging over, covering the damage and destruction with a ghostly veil. Despite this, the city was still at work, still busy with the clear-up, and earning a day's money to feed hungry bellies. No German bombers could destroy the spirit, the sheer life force of this unconquered city, my unconquered city. We were hardy souls, born of peoples who only a couple of generations earlier had left their home country of Ireland to seek food and shelter as famine ravaged their lands. We were survivors. And no matter how many bombs those Germans dropped on us, we'd come out unshaken and unbeaten.

Da had been at work, he couldn't bear to say any more farewells, and Nellie was looking after little Rita, so it was just me and him. I smiled a feeble smile, trying to jolly

Tommy along, but there was something sombre about our moods that refused to lighten with enforced gaiety.

We reached the water's edge. The day was cold and skies with heavy dusk-grey clouds lying low over the port. The *Arthur F. Corwin* tanker was magnificent in its way, a huge vessel that lay sprawling along the length of the dockyards. Two masts rose up over the main decks then a large funnel at one end and various operational sections jutting out over the cargo. It was surrounded by smaller vessels of differing sizes, and would move in convoy across the great swell of the Atlantic Ocean.

All at once I couldn't bear to see my brother board the ship. I tugged his arm and asked him to stop walking.

'What, our Maggie? I don't want to be late, like, or I'll get me arse kicked fer sure,' grinned Tommy. He put down the saddlebag he'd slung over his shoulder, and sensing my reserve, he hauled me into a hug.

'It won't be forever, girl. I'll be home safe and sound before ye know it,' he said, this time quietly.

I nodded my response. Something in me felt unsure. I bit my lip to stem the feeling inside me that he was too young to be heading into this war again. I didn't want him to go, but I definitely didn't want to blurt out my thoughts. We had to part on good terms, on confident terms. I didn't want to spook him before his trip had even begun, and sailors were notoriously superstitious.

'Stay safe out there, our Tommy,' I whispered. 'Yer've made us all so proud helpin' the war effort, but please be safe. Don't ye dare go near those German ships, or they'll have me to answer to.'

Tommy smiled at that, knowing I couldn't influence the U-boats, the bombers, the army, any more than I could fly. 'Time for me to go, girl. Keep Da and Rita safe, and our

Nellie, won't ye Maggie. It'll be sound, don't fret, like,' Tommy said, swinging his bag over his shoulder, giving me a last wink, and then heading off towards the ship.

I watched him go aboard, staying there on that wintry riverside for so long my lips felt blue with cold. Eventually, with a great bellow from the funnels, the vessel and all its scattered hangers on, moved with a lumbering grace out onto the river. I waved even though I knew it was unlikely Tommy would see me from the deck. The night was drawing in. Twilight was almost upon us. I turned to get the tram back to Latimer Buildings.

Days passed. Tommy's disappearance from our lives again created a hole at the centre of our family but we carried on, we had to. We sent him our nightly prayers, and our daily ones too, crossing ourselves a hundred times a day and fingering our rosaries. *Click clack. We want Tommy back.*

Night after night we listened for the siren that would mark the onset of the Luftwaffe, but nothing came. Perhaps the bombings had stopped? We could barely frame the thought, so afraid we were of being wrong, of having false hope. Then the night came when our hopes were well and truly smashed into smithereens; into shards that sliced through our community.

On the evening of 20 December, after Father, Nellie, Rita and I had eaten our sparse fare of mashed potato and barley stew, we settled into our beds early; me and Rita in the one single bed behind the curtain, Nellie in the other bedroom and Father in his chair by the range. Da popped his head round the curtain to give us goodnight, his braces hanging slack by his sides, one hand holding his trousers up at the back, the other holding a candle tray holding a lit wax taper. It was the only light in the room. My father wouldn't use the gas mantles because they popped and he didn't want the expense. With the blackout in force anyway, and our room in the heights of the tenement, we were plunged into an uneasy darkness.

I had no idea of the time beyond Father's last words that day, perhaps I had dozed off, but when the sound of the siren came it pierced into as-yet-unformed dreams with its eerie wail.

'Get up, get *up*!' I yelled, grabbing my dress and a cardie, and throwing them on. Nellie was instantly awake, her eyes wide with terror. 'The Germans are comin' fer us, get yer coat, get a blanket, we're goin' down to the shelter NOW.' I could hear the terror in my voice as the rolling, keening siren continued. I ran to Da, shaking him out of his slumbers. His face was creased into his dreaming, I pulled at his shirt until he startled awake. I didn't need to say any more. I pulled Nellie to the door and, with Rita wailing with fright in my arms, we raced down the steps with Da following. The four of us shot across the yard and into the Anderson shelter nearby.

We were meant to share it with five families but there was barely enough room for that many people so we couldn't be sure we'd fit. Several neighbours were already inside the construction: the Murphy family from the same tenement as us, four children and their parents. We crawled inside clutching our blankets and coats, knowing if we survived the night it would be a long, cold one, crammed in, freezing cold and terrified. Then just as I registered the eyes staring at me in the gloom, the first sounds reverberated overhead.

'Jaysus Christ,' moaned Mrs Murphy, a solidly built woman in her forties who looked older. Her face was lined, her brown hair thin and wispy. She was huddled in an old tartan coat with a scarf wrapped around the rollers in her hair.

Her husband, a thin, greying man who must've been a good five years older, sat next to her, not saying a word, sucking on his gums where his false teeth would have been. The four children were various ages from six years old to seventeen. All had white faces in the dark, bundled into their coats as we stared into an imaginary sky which was the roof of the tin and brick shelter, barely two feet above our heads.

The door opened as more people from the surrounding buildings crammed inside, all wide-eyed with fear. Among them was a priest. All eyes turned to him as he entered, reaching for some reassurance, some hope we'd survive the night perhaps. Sensing our desperation, his voice, thin at first, rose to intonate a prayer. We bowed our heads, listening, muttering the familiar words. What else could we do?

'Jesus do not leave me alone in suffering . . . Do not lessen any of my sufferings. Only give me the strength to bear them. Do with me as you please, Lord. Only give me the grace to be able to love you . . .'

Somewhere in the gloom a woman wept. We all chorused 'Amen' as the drone of the bombers intensified above our bowed heads. We looked up, nodding to each other as the thick, heavy throb of the engines sounded across the sky. Planes screamed above our heads, high-pitched moans raining down death and destruction upon us, the roar of the bombs exploding, getting ever nearer. Crashing, obliterating, smashing our city, our streets, our people.

Nellie clung to me, sobbing. All the while I was jiggling Rita in my arms as she screamed for dear life, trying without success to soothe her. I did what I could to reassure them both but there was nothing I could say. We were in God's hands, we had to trust and pray, that was all we could do.

Somehow we made it through that night, as we were hit by the start of what was later named the 'Christmas Blitz', an almighty assault the target of which was our Liverpool docks, so important were they to the national war effort. Wave after wave of attacks rained down on us by the Luftwaffe.

Then on 21 December came the fiercest night yet. Canada, Gladstone, Brocklebank, Princes, Wapping, Kings and Carrier docks were attacked. Several air raid shelters across the city were blasted into oblivion. People were dying while trying to keep their families safe. The loss of life was devastating. Across both north and south Liverpool, families lost their homes, their loved ones. It was horror of biblical proportions, and we were in the midst of it, somehow staying safe through the panic and terror.

On the night of the 22nd, the docks were hit again, this time Alexandra, Canada and Huskisson docks. We emerged from the three nights of sustained bombing to find our area changed beyond recognition. The town hall, Cunard offices and municipal buildings were all hit, becoming a raging furnace. The landing stage suffered a blow. A parachute mine had landed on Waterloo Dock, killing nine people in a single explosion. Houses were hit. Streets filled with ordinary people and their possessions, lain waste by the bombings.

Crawling out of the Anderson Shelter on the morning of 23 December, two days from that most Holy of days, Christmas Day, I surveyed our street in disbelief. Our tenements were still standing, though the air was thick with choking black smoke from the fires burning in the docklands. People were standing, staring at the buildings as if they could not believe their eyes.

I brushed my skirt down, and helped Nellie climb out, Rita clasped to my breast. We had survived but hundreds hadn't.

Today we had a home when hundreds hadn't. We may be dead tomorrow. We may be homeless tomorrow. Today was all we had. 'Better get the water on to boil, we'll need a cup of tea after that lot,' I said, turning to hold both Nellie's and Da's hand and smiling, Rita looking up at us, sucking her thumb. We were alive. We still had much to be grateful for.

With that, we went inside, determined not to fail in the face of the enemy, determined to carry on regardless.

CHAPTER 9

Tragedy Strikes

February 1941

Plumes of bitter incense formed a ghostly trail behind the priest and servers. I closed my eyes, taking in the familiar, sacred smell as the sound of chanting filled the church. This was my safe space, my haven from the toils of my daily life in wartime. I let the rituals wash over me, like cleansing baptism water, feeling for the presence of God within me.

The words from the Old Testament reading drifted in and out of my consciousness, but I couldn't tell you what the priest read that day. His words seemed to hum in the hush of the nave. I was exhausted of course from scrabbling around for rationed food, for making ends meet every week, from the back-breaking work I did from dawn till dusk. Usually, I listened to every word. It was something we learned to do from our school days, as the nuns at St Sylvester's would test us every Monday morning on which readings had been offered, to make sure we'd gone to Mass. And when it was a Holy Day of Obligation, when we were given a day off school to attend special Masses, well we wouldn't have dared miss those for fear of immediate divine retribution in the form of the nuns slapping our knuckles with those terrible rulers! Listening avidly was a habit that never left me, engaging completely with the ceremonies that marked my path through this small life. But today I felt so tired that the influence of those nuns and their strict ways fell away from me.

When it was time for me to join the congregation in the Liturgy of the Eucharist, the receiving of bread and wine as the body and blood of Christ, I knelt before the priest, a sigh escaping my lips as he placed the bread on my tongue, the wetness of Holy wine. It was a feeling like touching the miraculous, this part of Mass, the part where faith became certainty. I felt connected to God in that most intimate alchemy, that moment of transubstantiation. Flesh made substance.

It was a cold Sunday at the end of February 1941 and me, Da, Nellie and Rita were attending Mass at St Anthony's Church at the end of Scottie Road. It was a beautiful church, the walls decorated with colourful images of Christ's Passion, the light-filled chapel with the rows of simple wooden pews looking towards the altar with The Host in its ornate, golden surroundings.

I felt blessed sitting with my family, noting the gaps between people where their fathers, brothers and husbands used to be. Our congregation shrank weekly and the strength of our prayers increased in direct proportion. There wasn't a family around here who didn't have someone away fighting, and the pitch and camber of the services was felt more keenly than ever before. When Mass had ended, we filed out of the church, Da following behind me so he could push a ha'penny into the poor box by the door. He always put something in there even though we stood at the back, out of reach of the collection plate.

As we passed the statue of The Sacred Heart of Jesus I stopped to pick up a single candle, lighting it from the small bobbing flame of another, and slipping a ha'penny of my own into the slot of the box below the candle stand. Most of the candleholders were taken, lights burning with the hopes of loved ones for their menfolk, and all the people lost in the raids. I found a space and slotted the taper in, sending a small prayer for our Tommy, wherever he was.

'Dear Lord, keep him safe,' I whispered, touching the plaster hem of the statue of Jesus briefly, looking up into his face glowing in the candlelight. He was pulling open his white garment and pointing to his bleeding heart, his hand painted with the wound of the crucifixion, a single bead of colour representing the blood he spilled for us. His face was impassive, silent.

I needed the comfort my faith could bring me, but today I felt nothing except the seed of a growing sense of foreboding deep in my stomach. I crossed myself, turning away from the statue, picked up Rita who had watched my small ritual in awed silence, and followed other familiar faces out onto the small courtyard that fronted the building. Standing against the sandy-coloured exterior of the church we paused to chat with friends and neighbours before heading home. If I got the dinner on early I might be able to return for Benediction at 3 p.m. Setting down Rita to run and greet her friends, I watched my little girl with pride and not a little sadness. She was the spitting image of her father, with dark tresses and big eyes. I sighed, and smiled over at her as she turned for my nod of approval before the children all raced off together.

Da walked slowly today, the old injury to his foot causing him to wince as we went. Every now and then he'd reach down and pick up a stub of a cigarette or the discarded end of a roll-up. He'd place these carefully inside his baccy tin, scouting the ground for more 'treasures'.

'Go 'ed Da, the kids round here'll skit at yer again,' I admonished, knowing that Da had a nickname given by the feral children who teamed our busy streets. 'Yarbo, the nicker picker' they called him as a way of mocking his 'waste not, want not' attitude.

He didn't need a war on to know he had to make do and mend. The family joke was that my father could boil an egg and use the same water to make a cup of tea, he was so careful with money. And every night Da would take his snakeskin purse (I never did ask where he'd got that from, so incongruous it was to own something so exotic in the slums) and count his coins, laying them out on the bed. Every night, without fail, he'd check his money, then count them again just to make sure. But I didn't like the nickname. 'Yarbo' was our word for tramp. 'Nicker picker' being obvious, a joke about him picking up other peoples' discarded dead ends of cigarettes to make his own rollies.

Despite my caution, Da just laughed, saying he was saving a 'good few pennies' by being resourceful. I wasn't sure I liked his version of austerity as I didn't like our family being the object of jokes, but what could I do? Whatever made him happy. He'd had a hard enough life without me nagging him and spoiling the few pleasures he had. And being stone deaf had its advantages, he never actually heard the taunts of the local kids!

We hadn't been back at the garret on Latimer Street for more than ten minutes or so, I'd barely even pulled on my apron, when there was the sound of heavy footsteps on the stairs and a sharp rap at the door. I nudged Da and pointed over. He frowned then walked over to open it, just like any normal day, when there could be a neighbour wanting to borrow a cup of sugar behind it.

But it wasn't any of the housewives that lived in our court. It was two naval officers, dressed in full uniform of deepest blue with three gold stripes on their sleeves. One of the men carried a scroll and a small box. Da looked the men up and down, then gestured for them to enter, his face puzzled. Neither man took a step forward. Their faces were serious. Both then took off their hats, their smart military caps, holding them in front of them. Only one man spoke. For the life of me, I can't remember what he looked like, what either of them looked like, for in that instant I had guessed what they had come to tell us. I stared, transfixed, at that scroll of paper, that box, and I knew, I knew deep in my soul, that our beloved Tommy was never coming home to us.

It was clear my father hadn't yet understood. He looked confused more by the fact they hadn't come inside our drab home.

'Am I speaking to Mr Thomas Riley, father of Thomas Riley, who served with the Merchant Navy aboard the *Arthur F. Corwin?*' the man with the roll of paper, the box, spoke. He addressed his speech to Da but I was compelled to jump in and explain.

'Da's deaf as a doorpost, he can't hear you, like,' I cut in, 'but yes, he's Tommy's father, and our Tommy's me brother.' My voice sounded younger than my twenty years, a girlish, rather high-pitched tremor that registered the fear I was now feeling. The officer turned to me, unfurled the roll of paper and began to read, his voice a calm, firm tone settling into our silence.

Despite the fact that Da couldn't hear, his face confirmed that he'd guessed the terrible truth that was about to hit us with the force of a tornado. It was bleached as white as the alabaster saints of our church, and for a moment I thought he might faint.

I held the back of a wooden chair, suddenly feeling giddy myself. The room swam in front of my eyes. In those brief seconds, I had a vision of life before this conversation, and how it would never, ever, be the same again. I wished I could hold onto that second before the news, and stay there, so I could live without ever having to hear the words that ripped the heart out of my family forever.

'Mr Riley. It is with the deepest regret that I have learned that your son, Mr Thomas Riley, who was serving in the Merchant Navy, has been recorded as supposed drowned whilst on service with his ship.

'By command of His Majesty the King the names of those members of the Merchant Navy who have given their lives in the service of their country are recorded in the Merchant Navy Roll of Honour. I am now adding Mr Riley's name to the Roll of Honour, and as I do so, wish to express my admiration for the services he rendered and to convey to you and your family my profound sympathy in your sad bereavement . . .'

While the officer was reading, Da turned to me, and I nodded. I felt seized by shock, my legs started to tremble and in that moment I wanted to run away from this scene of utter devastation. I don't know where I'd have gone, I just wanted to get as far away from this room, this news, this avalanche of pain as I could. I gripped the back of the chair tighter to keep myself upright. Whatever happened I had to be the one who witnessed this, for my father's sake, for our Nellie's sake as well. The words sank into me. Our Tommy was gone from us. His body was somewhere at sea in the broiling depths of the Atlantic, lost to us forever. There would be no grave except the watery depths. There could be no place to mark his life. Along with hundreds of others, he had perished at sea and we would have to learn how to live without him. In that moment I thought I'd never feel happiness or joy ever again. I couldn't see how we get through this, how we'd manage our lives without our cheeky, naughty, lovely boy, even though he was a man now, and he'd died a man's death, a wartime death.

When the officer had finished speaking, he placed his hat back on his head with a gesture of timeless respect for the bereaved. He straightened it, then turned to Da and handed him the box. Neither Da nor I had spoken. Nellie was away outside somewhere with one of her friends with Rita, both oblivious to the tragedy unfolding in our lives and I was glad it was so. They had precious extra minutes of normality, without the new guest we'd welcomed in, the grief that would sit with us from this day onwards, suffocating us, owning us.

The officers shut the door as they left. There was silence, the kind of absence of sound that exists in the split seconds before a shell explodes. Then the air was rent by a moan of total despair, of horror beyond imagining. Da's face was contorted in a spasm of loss and love – the bleak, dark anger of grief. With a howl I have only ever heard from an animal in pain, he hurled the box and its contents at the closed doorway and sank to his knees, keening into the rawness of his emotions, yet another grieving parent, yet another family devastated by this dreadful war.

I ran to him, holding his head, trying to contain his anguish, but it fought with my own. The pain inside me reared up and I joined his terrible lament. Tears came, fresh and hot on my cheeks. I held him, feeling the shuddering waves of heartbreak engulf us both.

We stayed like that until, wiping his face, Da rose up and shuffled, bent over, to his chair. He turned his face from me, somehow ashamed of his outburst of natural feeling. It was then I spotted the contents of the box, a medal with a brightly coloured ribbon lying on the floor. I crawled over to it, picking it up as tenderly as I would a newborn child, cradling the only visible, real connection we had left of our brother. I looked over the silver disc, brushing off imaginary dirt.

It was a War Medal, issued for 28 days of service. It had a lion standing on a double-headed dragon on one side, and the crowned effigy of King George VI on the other, with a red, blue and white striped ribbon. It had a single oak leaf clasp to signify a Mention in Despatches. Our only legacy of Tommy's short life.

'He died a war hero, Da,' I sniffed, stroking his arm, gazing at the medal in my hand that my brother had won for king and country, 'he died a hero.'

Da wouldn't turn his face back to meet mine. His silence said everything. His heart was broken, possibly beyond repair. How could that symbol of Tommy's sacrifice ever be enough to comfort us? It represented a life wiped out too soon, no more than that. I was proud of Tommy, of course I was, but the pain was too raw, too harsh, to feel anything but rage at that sparkling medallion which embodied everything we had lost.

I could see my father retreat into himself like he had when Mam left us. Would we lose our father as well as our brother? Would he be lost to us in grief?

The next few days were a blur, I can barely recall how we managed to eat, sleep and cope. Even though Rita was only a toddler, too young to understand the tragedy that had stricken the heart of our family, I was sure she sensed the shift that had taken place. I tried hard to carry on as normal, keeping my tears to myself and only letting them fall freely when Rita was asleep. But even so, she was unsettled, walking around after my da, following him with her arms outstretched, asking for cuddles, and knowing he had retreated from us all.

Telling Nellie was the hardest thing I'd ever had to do. It was clear that Da was unable to frame the words. My thirteen-year-old sister nodded gravely, her understanding surpassing her young years, but her tears came as well and we cried together, holding each other and wailing for our beloved brother.

By evening, it seemed the whole neighbourhood knew of our Tommy's death. Many had seen the gleaming navy car pull up outside our court. It was a sight we all feared, knowing there was only one reason the large, expensive vehicles would venture down our way. Neighbours and friends started to arrive. Mrs Corrigan, a small fierce woman from the ground floor, in black skirts and the ubiquitous apron, came with a simple stew for our dinner. One of the Murphy children, a teenage boy called James, arrived with a loaf of brown bread for our breakfast. People came in and out of our flat with condolences, sympathy, food and concern, but it went past me in a daze of sorrow. I couldn't for the life of me piece together those first few days after we learned of Tommy's demise.

We didn't have details of the sinking of the *Arthur F. Corwin* for weeks, perhaps months, afterwards, and I forget even now how we learned the full extent of the maritime tragedy. But learn it, in time, we did. Forty-six sailors lost their lives when the *Arthur F. Corwin* tanker was torpedoed by two separate German U-boats. The ship was sailing back on its perilous Atlantic journey to Avonmouth with a cargo of 10,000 tons of aviation fuel to supply the allied forces fighting in Europe. It was two days off the British coast when disaster struck.

It left Halifax, Canada, on 30 January 1941, in a convoy of forty-one ships, protected by three Royal Navy battleships and several smaller escort vessels. Unbeknown to us, Liverpool was scheduled to become the new allied command centre for Western Approaches, making the city port top of the strategic targets for Hitler. The seas were, by all accounts, a raging cauldron of thirty-foot waves as storms battered the vessels. U-boats had been spotted 200 miles south-east of their position so perhaps they knew it was only a matter of time before German forces hit at the core of the British military mission, and so they did, on the afternoon of Thursday, 13 February. At 4.25 p.m., Greenwich Mean Time, U-103 damaged the tanker with two torpedoes, leaving it in flames, though missing the vast tanks holding the fuel cargo.

The radio operator had sent out a Mayday distress signal before the boat was hit a second time at 7.50 p.m., this time breaching the aviation fuel tanks. As U-96 sent two more torpedoes, the tanker exploded with mighty force, belching great black smoke into the night sky as molten metal fell, causing the turgid sea itself to burn.

Rescue crafts were on their way, but the freezing waters claimed its next victim as the ship sank. The ship master, forty-four crew members, including our eighteen-year-old Tommy, and one gunner were all killed. There were no survivors. All perished in a terrible slaughter that marked the turning point in our lives.

From that day onwards, with Nellie and Rita tucked in beside me, I don't recall a night I didn't go to sleep without hearing the sound of our father weeping. Da was a changed man. He'd always been serious and gentle, a personality honed by bitter experience and hard knocks, but he withdrew from us, consumed by the loss of his only son. Every single night he sobbed for our boy. And there was nothing I could do to take away his pain, as it was the pain we all felt.

There was also no funeral to attend and organise, no rites to mark his passing as he'd died at sea. We had no place to visit, nowhere to plant flowers and talk to our boy, hoping against hope that somewhere at God's right hand he'd hear our whispers. Without a body to bury, he was lost to us in ways more profound even than death. We had no closure, no completion of the act of dying, just a nagging sense of the unreachable nature of losing someone we loved.

I spoke to Tommy in my mind each day. Things would happen, Everton would win or lose, and I'd want to tell him, so I'd half-turn then realise he wasn't there, he'd never be there again, so instead I'd have the conversation in my head. At times, I wondered if I was going mad with grief. But even that contact with my deceased brother brought me some measure of relief. I was sure he could hear me, wherever he was, my love for him was so strong I couldn't see how he wouldn't. Love goes beyond physicality, beyond our imagining. I drew on the strength of Christ's Passion for that. How He was reborn in a miracle that went beyond ordinary human understanding. And while I didn't expect our Tommy to be resurrected in anything except the love in our hearts, I took comfort from my religion in this, our darkest hour.

One morning, I took myself down to Pier Head to scan the bomb-ravaged docks and the grey ever-moving river that lead to the ocean. I wanted to feel some solid connection with Tommy by going, and some consolation perhaps. But the waves tipped with white from the wind that howled that bleak winter brought me nothing, the swirling undercurrents revealing nothing. I wanted to find Tommy there, but there was no sign of him, no special revelation and so I turned away, bitter disappointment etched into my soul. He'd gone from us, and there was no way to call him back.

CHAPTER 10

Evacuation

May 1941

The train gave a great whistle, belching plumes of black smoke into the air at Lime Street Station. I grabbed two-year-old Rita's hand and half-dragged her to the waiting engine with Nellie by my side carrying her pillowcase containing her meagre things. We'd been told by the authorities to pack only a few bits each; a tin or two of spam, condensed milk and some jam butties, as well as a vest, pair of pants, a jumper, two pairs of socks and, of course, our regulation gas mask. My best friend Lizzy, who had married a seaman three years earlier, raced along beside me with her two-year-old son, Jimmy, as the queue of people being evacuated from Liverpool snaked through the station.

'Come 'ed our Lizzy, we want to get ourselves a seat!' I hollered, reaching the door and lifting Rita up into the carriage. We all had our gas masks carried round our necks with string in a small brown cardboard box and little enough else. It was a bright, sunny day and we'd boarded a special bus laid on by those same authorities to bring us to the station, bidding farewell to those of our neighbours who had chosen to remain in our streets, despite the regular onslaughts by the Luftwaffe.

The bombing raids intensified after we learned of Tommy's death. It was only just over a week ago, on 25 April 1941, that Winston Churchill, our Prime Minister, had visited Liverpool, and we wondered if Hitler had got wind of it and sent his fighters in retaliation. I wish I'd been there to see him. I'd been too busy with chores and mouths to feed to go into the centre of town to witness such a historic moment, but I knew plenty of people round here who had.

Paddy, a local ragamuffin who lived in the tenement opposite ours, recounted his story from the day the nation's leader came to visit. Surrounded by a group of other residents; children, young and old women with their baskets of washing, carrying babes in arms or shooing children from one place to another, all stopped to listen to our own raconteur. Paddy, who was a good looking lad of fifteen, had hopped onto a tram and into town to see the spectacle. He told us there were crowds four or five people deep, waving flags and calling to Churchill. The roads were lined with policemen, some were mounted on horseback, some on foot. As Churchill's black car drove into view the crowds went wild. The man himself stood at the back of the vehicle, one hand aloft holding his black hat, his face impassive, stern.

'Ye couldn't hear yerself think it were so loud, like,' said Paddy, his eyes glowing as he recounted his tale, 'and it were full of people, so many people, I could hardly breathe in them crowds!'

At this he looked delighted. Boys like him saw the visit as a chance to see something new, be involved in something exciting and important, but for us as a city it meant so much more than that. We knew our docks were vital to the war effort but we wanted to be told we were important, that our city mattered, and Churchill coming did just that. To crowds of rapturous applause, the great man had said those famous words that had struck a chord in every Scouse heart in the city: 'I see the damage done by the enemy attacks but I also see the spirit of an unconquered people.'

*

Then, a few days later, on 3 May 1941, Mill Road Hospital was hit, killing a maternity ward full of new mothers and babies. Then Scottie Road suffered an almighty shelling, the explosion reverberating around our narrow streets.

It was then that Da looked at me and said, 'It's time fer ye to go, pet.'

I nodded. We'd seen plenty of other families be evacuated, and we couldn't think of leaving our home and neighbours, but something had changed. Life felt more fragile and precious than ever, and so, reluctantly, I agreed to leave.

Da, who was too old and too maimed by his various injuries to be conscripted, had refused point blank to come with us, saying he wouldn't be able to find work elsewhere. He said he'd be a fish out of water and he'd rather work and face the Germans in Liverpool than scratch around for a living somewhere else. Even though it was he who urged us to go, I hated leaving him.

As I'd hugged him tightly goodbye at the bus stop, my small suitcase sitting on the ground next to me, I'd smelled his homely warmth, that mixture of soot, sweat and spices that would forever remind me of him. Though I understood why he chose to stay living among the bomb-ravaged wreckage of north Liverpool, I still begged him to come, one last time. 'Da, don't stay here. Come with us, please let us all go together ...' There were tears in my eyes as I'd held my cheek against his stocky chest.

I could hear him wheezing as he'd replied: 'No, pet, I'm no good anywhere but here. You keep me girls safe.'

He'd been coughing on and off since our Tommy died, his illness lingering on and on as his grief-stricken body failed to fight off the infection. Even though Da couldn't hear a word of what I said, he squeezed me tighter, and in that gesture I knew he'd understood, but I also knew he wouldn't change his mind.

With a sob, I let him go. We queued for the bus with other familiar faces. Well, everyone was familiar! We all spoke to each other, friends, neighbours and strangers alike. We had no airs, nor graces. Our humanity was what made us Scousers legendary, that and our dry sense of humour that showed our spirit was unbeatable against all the odds being thrown at us by life, especially now.

'We're off on our 'olidays,' deadpanned a grandmother who was waiting alongside us to wave off her daughter and three grandchildren.

'Yeah, it's a Jerry Away Day, like!' I replied, chuckling.

'Don't let those German bastards spoil yer trip,' added another woman standing with two tussling children at her feet.

'Them Germans have got nothin' to do with it, we've been plannin' a visit to a farm in the arse end of Wales or Scotland or Timbuctoo, wherever they're sendin' us, for ages!' I laughed back.

There was something surreal about this 'outing', like we really were about to go on a day trip, rather than the reality of fleeing those Jerries and their death machines in the sky. None of us knew when, or if, we'd be back home, or if home would still be standing.

I couldn't take my eyes off Da because I knew that staying here, in these dockland streets, was tantamount to a death sentence, and that as sure as God existed then there would be more carnage, more visitations from hell, possibly tonight, possibly every night until this terrible war was over. Me da looked worn out. His hair, always a shocking white, looked straggly and thin, his grey skin was covered in stubble, which he would never have let grow before. He stooped, which, adding to his limp and his deafness, made him resemble a man of seventy rather than the fifty-seven-year-old he was. He wasn't old, but he looked defeated. Even now, nearly three months after Tommy's death, he still cried himself to sleep every night, though none of us dared say a word about it. Nellie and I pretended not to hear him. We didn't want to add yet more injury to his loss, but it pained us deeply.

As we boarded the bus, I blew him a kiss and held Rita up to wave at him. How do we express love in a few short words and gestures? I hope I'd shown him what my heart was filled with. He must've known, but the untimely and tragic passing of his son had stolen something from him, something of his essential humanity, his peace, which deep down I didn't think he'd ever recover.

I was musing on this as the bus pulled away from the kerb and rumbled through the devastated streets. I looked around, shocked into silence. I had not travelled this way in months. Buildings that once towered over the narrow roads and thoroughfares now lay in splintered, desiccated piles, obliterated and empty, their ceilings and floors gone, sliced away, leaving behind frail carcasses of metal and brick. Dust lay thick, spewed from the flames and crumbling masonry, while shredded wallpaper held together sections of bricks in a forlorn, tattered mess. Our city was unrecognisable.

We passed groups of 'gawpers', or so we called them, elderly women and children chatting, grouping together with tales of other worse-damaged sites to inspect. There was a sense of disbelief; this was so far out of our ordinary lives that it was almost like being asleep with a nightmare unfolding that would never end, and would contain us all for eternity.

*

The train station was busy with officials with clipboards with queues of children and their mothers. The Pied Piper Operation of September 1939 had meant that children were originally evacuated in their school-loads without their frantic mothers, sent off on the steam trains with their pillow cases of possessions and perhaps a sandwich for the journey. Those women never knew where their children were going, or whether they'd see them again, and as a mother I shuddered at the thought. We'd all seen the pictures in the local rag, boys in long shorts, girls with ribbons in their hair, wearing their gas masks with a label tied round them, being sent off into the unknown. How must they have felt? Everyone had been so brave, and now it was our turn, just thank Our Lord we were together.

The journey was a pleasant one, though long, and we stared out of the window as the cityscape vanished and fields rolled before us. Cows and trees, and huge, huge skies above our heads. Well we'd never seen anything like it! I'd never seen a real cow in my life, and neither had Nellie or Rita.

'It's a moo cow! A proper moo cow!' exclaimed my Rita with glee, her nose pressed up to the glass of the window.

'It sure is, our Rita, aren't they big, like?' I smiled back, almost as eagerly, 'an' there are so many of them!'

The fields seemed to stretch forever. It was such a contrast to the narrow courts and alleys of our blackened streets.

The more miles were placed between us and home, the more I felt a sickening in my stomach. Already I missed the familiar sights and sounds, the cobbled roads, the trams and bustling docks. There would be no whiff of tobacco from the roll-ups smoked on the streets, no reek of the burning factories or the spices each time the docks were hit, and perhaps there'd be no squalor, no lice, no queuing for our rations of bread and milk either.

It was dusk by the time we arrived at a place called Nantwich in Cheshire, our fingers sticky from the bags of sweets given out to the children by kindly helpers on the train. I felt that sinking feeling again as we disembarked, holding Rita and Nellie's hands as much to contain my own fears as to comfort theirs. Lizzy and Jimmy stood beside us, and we glanced over at each other, our faces pale with tiredness and uncertainty. We stood on a platform that seemed so small besides our Lime Street ones, a bundle of stragglers who didn't belong out here among the fields and all that green grass we'd seen from the train.

A woman with yet another clipboard was marking off names, and as they did so, people would come forward, a kindly looking matron with horn-rimmed spectacles, a proud looking man wearing a suit with a trilby, and evacuees would walk off with them to their new, hopefully temporary, homes, until everyone had been accounted for except us. We stood, holding hands, our suitcases and Rita's pillowcase stuffed with her doll and clothes, at our feet. My daughter yawned a great big yawn then turned to me, holding her hands up to me. I picked her up, suddenly fearful that someone would try and separate us. 'We stick together, no matter what they say,' I whispered to Lizzy, and she nodded back at me. There was no way I was letting anyone split us up.

'Margaret McGee, I take it that's you?' said the billeter, who had been marking off names. She looked over her board at me, raising her eyebrows.

'Yes, that's me, and this is our Nellie and my daughter Rita, our Lizzy and her boy Jimmy. We're together and that's how we'll stay,' I replied firmly, suddenly feeling self-conscious of my Liverpudlian accent when the women spoke so 'posh' in her northern lilt.

'We're just waiting for yours to arrive, Mrs McGee. You'll

be staying together so there's no need to worry. You'll be at the Bennet's farm a few miles from here. Mrs Bennet will collect you but she's rather late I'm afraid.'

With that the women clucked her teeth in disapproval and looked back at her papers. She'd been kind, though, not separating us and putting my main fear to rest, and I appreciated that even though she was a little 'stuck-up', as we'd say in our street.

'Nothing to do but wait,' she added, rather unnecessarily I thought.

'Mam, I'm hungry,' wailed Rita. The day had simply been too much for her and she was starting to get fractious.

I shushed her. 'Now then our Rita, we won't have long to wait and we'll go to the farmhouse. I'm sure there'll be a good dinner waitin' fer us, like,' I promised, not feeling at all sure that this would be the case but wanting to reassure my little one. We had no food left except for a couple of tins so there was nothing I could give her. There was nothing to do but wait and hope I was right. Nellie pointed to a bench and so we all sat down, the last evacuees on the platform waiting for the next stage of this drama to play out.

Eventually a woman in a rough workday jacket and very muddy trousers clomped onto the platform leaving a trail of dirt from her wellington boots. Nellie and I looked at each other. *Please God this isn't her,* I prayed to myself. But it was. I'd never seen a woman wearing trousers before, and the sight of her almost made me bark out loud with laughter. I suppressed my reaction, but nudged Lizzy all the same, knowing she'd be as flabbergasted as I was. If the lady noticed, she paid no attention to us.

With a whistle, and barely a word exchanged, this bizarre woman herded us to her farm vehicle and we chugged off out of the small town centre. Before long the quaint streets and pretty houses vanished leaving us weaving down uneven tracks as darkness fell. The air smelled odd, of animals, a sour tang that made Lizzy exclaim, 'I'd rather the soot in my lungs than cow shit!'

We giggled at that, but the farmer said nothing except to sniff her disapproval. Just then the truck ground to a halt, and we all jolted forward, nearly losing Rita from my lap as she was almost asleep. Without a word, we descended from the vehicle, looking around us, trying to make shapes out of the dark night.

The sky seemed vast, with more stars in it than I'd seen in my life, even on nights as a child when I'd scrambled down to the docks to watch the ferries come and go. No, this was completely different. The sky was black, the stars were like a rash lying across it, and the land was a dense haze of low-lying buildings. I could make out nothing else in the gloaming. A dog barked, and we all jumped again.

'Follow me,' said Mrs Bennet. She was a small, wiry woman with brown short hair and a manly way of walking. She looked like she'd suffer no mischief, we'd have to behave ourselves, that much was apparent!

She wasn't unkind to us. She walked us through the back door of her cottage into a warm kitchen, with a fire glowing in the range and the smell of porridge coming from a pot set aside from the cooking heat.

'You'll help yourselves,' was all she said, before pointing to the stairs at the back of the room and telling us our room was there waiting for us, and we'd need to be up early for a 7 a.m. start in the fields. Then she vanished into the bowels of the building, taking her mangy collie dog trailing after her.

Lizzy and I looked at each other, struck dumb. It hadn't

occurred to me that we'd have to work for our supper, literally!

'I'm not touchin' no, cows, or sheep for that matter!' I blurted out.

Then Lizzy and I looked at each other, standing in a stranger's kitchen with the prospect of a day doing God-knows-what on a farm in the middle of nowhere, and we burst into laughter. I hadn't laughed so much in ages. It must have been a mixture of exhaustion, worry and a sense of the ridiculous, and once started we couldn't stop.

We laughed and laughed, holding onto the backs of the wooden chairs in that cosy farmhouse room, with our children looking at us with bemused faces until they finally joined in the merriment.

'Oh sweet Mary,' I sighed, wiping the tears of happiness from my eyes, 'I haven't had a good belly ache like that since I don't know when.'

'Me neither, our Maggie,' said Lizzy, rubbing her sides and complaining, 'I've done meself an injury from all the hilarity.'

'We'd best get some porridge inside us if we're to be up and milking cows tomorrow,' I added, and we collapsed once more into loud guffaws.

And yet the joke was on me, on all of us. The next morning, after we'd all trooped out of our beds after snatching a few hours' restless sleep, yawning into the grey early morning as the cocks crowed and the sheep baaed and the cows made their low insistent noise, we discovered that milking cows was exactly what our farmer's wife had in store for us.

The children were left to play in the grass, tearing through the hedgerows and around the filthy, mud-streaked pens until they were as dirty as their surroundings. Free as birds they played as Nellie watched over them, leaving Lizzy and me to do the hard graft that was expected of us in return for bed and board. It wasn't much of a bed, we each had one iron bed for our respective families, but we'd survived worse. Then there was the porridge again for breakfast, but we'd also had little or nothing some days at home so anything hot was a welcome sight.

But the farm work, well that was something I didn't like, not at all! I was a city girl, born and raised in urban streets with factories, warehouses, horses pulling carts, and humanity, in one busy, dirty melee. I didn't know, or care, how a farm was run, or how people lived in the countryside. Being set down in Cheshire was akin to being sent to Mars for me, and I admit I hated every second of it. The place smelled bad, of fresh manure which made me feel like gagging at so early a time in the morning. The fields were green, the trees were green, the sky was grey, there was no colour, no noise, no bustle.

'Where in the hell have we landed?' whistled Lizzy, reading my mind as we stood at the kitchen door waiting for Mrs B., as we called her, to show us our first tasks.

The woman, who must have been in her early fifties but looked sprightly and fit, strode ahead of us, saying, 'Follow me.' And so we did. To the cow shed. 'Holy Jaysus!' Lizzy exclaimed, 'we're goin' to have to milk those cows, I know it.'

'Language Lizzy, stop yer blaspheming!' I countered, but I knew she was right. We followed behind Mrs B., walking gingerly through the mud and goodness knows what else.

'Me shoes'll be ruined,' I whispered as we entered, a slurry of manure and hay on the ground.

'Revoltin'!' mouthed Lizzy, holding her nose.

I would've laughed again but I was too taken aback by the rich odour coming from the line of cows moaning as they waited for their daily milking.

'Here's the bucket. Kneel down there and I'll show you how it's done,' barked the farmer.

'Ye go first, I can't do it,' said Lizzy, nudging me forward.

Reluctantly I knelt into the sludge and watched as the farmer grabbed the teats that seemed to pulse in her hand. With swift strong strokes she released the steaming stream of white liquid into the tin bucket.

'You have a go, go on give it a try,' smiled Mrs B. She was finally taking pity on us, but not enough to stop the rather traumatic lesson in milking. I shifted a little, thought, *What the heck!*, and bent down, grabbing a teat and making the cow totter slightly on her feet.

'Slowly, don't frighten her,' soothed Mrs B., taking hold of my hands and showing me how to do it. The milk soon splashed into the bucket, and even though I felt a small sense of pride in accomplishing my first task, I was still utterly disgusted by the experience.

Then Mrs B. stood up, wiped her hands on her overalls and said with a brusque smile that we would need to finish the lot of them before noon.

'We have to milk all of them?' wailed Lizzy, her face aghast.

Again, that small smile from our landlady. 'By noon, please, best get cracking.' And with that, the farmer walked out, whistling for her dog as she went, leaving Lizzy and me staring at each other in horror.

That night, we sat talking at the small window of the poky little room in the eaves that we shared. Nellie, Rita and Jimmy were all fast asleep, their faces pink from chasing around outside all day. They loved being here, in direct contrast to our feelings, but even today Jimmy had piped up, asking when we were going home.

'I don't want to stay here.' My voice was flat. I was feeling tearful after a second tiring day. I hated pretty much everything about our situation here, but mostly I hated being away from Da. I missed him with every bone in my body. How would I know if he ate a proper supper without me there to cook it for him? How would I know if he'd go to Mass without me on his arm, proudly showing me off to his pals from the dockyards? He had no one to darn his socks or pull off his jacket after an eighteen-hour day carrying heavy sacks, and no one to pour him a cup of steaming hot tea, or roll one of his dog-end ciggies. No, I wanted to go home and my mind was made up.

'I'm not stayin' a minute longer, our Lizzy. I can't bear thinking of Da all alone in Liverpool with no one to help him.'

'Shhh, our Maggie, it'll seem better in the mornin', yer'll see. We've got to stay. They're bombing Liverpool to bits and we'd be in danger being there. Come on now, ye wouldn't want Rita or Nellie to get hurt, would ye?' Lizzy knew how to soothe me, but also how to make me stay. I knew that Lizzy hated being here with a passion that matched my own, but she was also the more practical of us two. I knew if anyone was going to make the decision to stay or leave, it would be me.

Of course I didn't want my daughter or sister hurt, or worse, in the bombing raids, but I also knew that I wanted us all to be together, through thick and thin, and if it meant living with the prospect of a few blasted German bombs then so be it.

'I trust in God to keep us safe,' I said stoutly, though the natural answer would've been that God wasn't looking when our Tommy needed Him. But Lizzy didn't say it, and I chose not to think it. Tommy was in God's hands now, by His side, and who was I to question God's will?

'If God wants us to live, we'll live. If not . . .' I paused, I didn't even want to say the words.

'Well, let's give it a week. Just one week and if you still feel the same at the end of it, we'll go home. I can't stand it here meself, all them cows mooing all day and the bloody chickens waking us up too early'

Lizzy smiled her sweet smile at me, her lovely face lit softly by moonlight. 'I miss our home too. Give me the smell of the court lavvies over a pig pen any day,' she guffawed, and we both collapsed into giggles.

'All right, a week. But promise me that if I still feel the same way we'll go home?' I pleaded.

Lizzy reached for my hand, holding it in hers. Turning her green eyes towards me she said, 'I promise, our Maggie. If we both feel the same way after a week, then I'll race you to the station!'

Every morning for that next seven days, we woke to the sound of the cock crowing at 4 a.m. We ate our small portions of porridge, rubbing our bleary eyes and exhaling as we started our miserable daily chores. By the end of each day we were tired, aching and very, very dirty. We washed ourselves down as best we could using the outside water pump, then treated ourselves to a soak in the kitchen, pouring boiling kettles of water into the tin bath and shrieking as we splashed our mucky children once it had cooled.

Despite the week passing, my ache for my home city, and for my father, only worsened. On the last day of our agreed time limit, things came to a head. I had been left to milk the cows by myself as Lizzy was feeding scraps to the pigs, and I had two great containers filled to the brim with fresh milk to show for my efforts. I picked up one in each hand and started making my way back to the farmhouse to present to Mrs B. when I slipped on a patch of mud on the slippery concrete yard. I went head over heels, casting the frothing liquid in an arc spanning the courtyard, and landing on my bottom with an inelegant thud. Milk dripped down my apron, into my boots, and with a sob I shouted, 'That's it, we're done here, I'm goin' home!'

Without a murmur of objection from Lizzy or the children, we packed up our things and left the next morning. Mrs B. was good enough to drive us back to Nantwich Station where we got the first train heading back to Liverpool. Sinking back into the seats, Lizzy and I roared with laughter, grateful to be away from that draughty old farmhouse, and to be returning where we belonged.

The fields and lanes, the sky and lowing cows, all disappeared without trace as the outline of buildings came into view. The closer we got to our city, the pall of smoke hung over us, the lacerated buildings rising into view. Despite the impression of a place smashed into irreconcilable pieces, I didn't see any of it. I saw a place rising from the ashes, a place where people looked after each other, where the little we had was shared. I saw a city under assault and I wanted to be there, despite the danger, the terrible gut-wrenching risks. I wanted to be with my father, keeping our family close by me.

My eyes stung as we stepped down off the train, the strain of the journey and the smoke from the burning buildings forcing us to blink and wipe our faces. None of it mattered. *Whatever lies ahead, whatever challenges or fears, we will face them together as a family should.*

With that thought I hauled our luggage up, grabbed Rita's hand and marched forwards to find if our tenement was still standing, to learn if our father was still alive. For the first time in seven long days I felt that precious feeling of home equating with love thudding through my chest.

CHAPTER 11

Courting Again

June 1941 – 10 January 1942

'Don't ye look the bee's knees!' laughed my friend Flora. 'Give us a twirl then!'

I grinned sheepishly, spinning round to show my pals my Sunday best dress, which was my favourite periwinkle blue. It fitted perfectly around my figure and tapered into a soft flare with the skirt, which if I say so myself, showed off my slim legs and new high-heeled shoes a treat. I had also curled my shiny brown hair and slicked on a daub of lipstick, which felt incredibly daring. I was a young woman of twenty, in my prime, and ready to enjoy myself away from my usual responsibilities at home. It wasn't often I got the chance to have a night out with Lizzy and the Pendleton's Ices girls, who were kind enough to invite me out with them even though I didn't work there. Lizzy had got her old job back as soon as we'd returned to Liverpool. Pendleton's Ices were crying out for women to work as so many had left to join the war effort.

'Will I do?' I smiled. I felt like a Hollywood actress all glammed up to the nines for our night out at a local dance. It was a warm Saturday night at the start of June in 1941 and me, Lizzy, Flora and a couple of other girls who also worked together at the ice cream factory, were running late for the tram that would take us into the centre of Liverpool.

'Come 'ed, Judy Garland. Pick those heels up or we'll miss our ride!' exclaimed Lizzy, grabbing my arm and pulling me up the road.

I wasn't used to walking in heels and I felt like a bit like a newborn deer, wobbling daintily on the cobbles, trying not to break my ankles. I was grateful for her arm to cling on to as the streets were thronged with people; packs of lads and lasses, and young courting couples, off out to enjoy precious time away from the ships and the trenches and the factories, away from the realities of wartime Britain. And who could blame them? Life was precarious and dangerous. None of us knew if we'd see tomorrow, so why not make the most of the time we had, with family, friends and, of course, with the young officers and seamen who brought such poignant urgency to their courting.

'I'd better stick to one port and lemon tonight or I'll break me leg in these shoes,' I shouted above the noise of the tram, as it rattled through our blackened streets.

Lizzy looked a beauty as usual, standing tall next to us in a soft pink dress with her dark hair hanging down her back. I sighed as I watched her. I could never feel jealous of her as she was too nice for that, but I'd always wondered how it would be to have long lustrous hair like hers. We chuckled and joked, giggled and messed, about, until eventually we hopped off the tram, Flora giving the conductor a cheeky wink as she went.

'If there's an air raid tonight, girls, ye just come lookin' fer me,' hollered the conductor, who was old enough to be a father to any one of us. 'I'll look after yous all!' he finished.

'Dirty arl bugger,' laughed Flora again, tossing her brown curly hair. She nudged me, then skipped in front of our gaggle of curls, lipstick and high-pitched excitement.

Queuing outside the dance hall, Lizzy and I were chatting when I looked up into the crowds of young people. Standing only a few feet from me was perhaps the most handsome man I'd ever set eyes on. He was dressed in a seaman's uniform and stood at least half a head taller than the others. He had blonde hair and a way of standing that looked like he owned the world! For a moment I was stunned, as he caught my eye and I hastily looked away. What would he think of me, looking for all the world like I was trying to flirt with him? I was naturally shy with men, and would never have made a move on a chap, my morals and strict upbringing forbade any of that nonsense. But he'd made an impression on me, and I looked back quizzically, wondering why he'd noticed me, and as I did I realised he was staring over at me again.

'Lizzy,' I whispered urgently, 'stand there in front of me.'

'Why, Maggie, what are ye up to?' whispered back Lizzy.

'Just do it, please,' I hissed.

'All right, I'm movin' ye crazy cow,' sighed Lizzy, who burst into giggles, 'but I bet I know why, I spotted him too, he's a looker all right.'

'Shhhhh, our Lizzy, don't let him hear ye speak like that!' I begged, turning scarlet.

'He's all right, isn't he?' one of the other girls snorted, 'I saw him lookin' at ye, Maggie, looks like yer've made a conquest already tonight.'

'Shhh, Jean, I don't know what ye mean. I'm not lookin' fer a fella tonight or any other night,' I stammered, getting more and more flustered, casting my eyes to the ground with the shame of it. 'Come on, the queue's moving,' I said with some relief.

As I spoke I caught Lizzy smiling at me kindly. She knew I'd been left with emotional scars after Thomas McGee's desertion of me and our baby daughter, whether by death or neglect I still had no idea. Even though officially I was a married woman, I'd had neither sight nor sound, nor even a letter, from Thomas since the day after our wedding three years' earlier. To be honest, I assumed he was dead now. I didn't expect to hear from him ever again, but that didn't stop me feeling that I was better off on my own. I had Da, and our Rita and Nellie to care for, and that was enough for me, thank you very much, and I said as much to my friends. I knew they meant well and it was just a bit of teasing, but things were obviously still a bit raw where my feelings for the opposite sex were involved.

'All right, all right, our Maggie, we didn't mean to upset ye,' soothed Lizzy. 'Come 'ed, we'll lose our place in the queue an' all if we don't stop natterin' and get inside, we don't want to miss the dance.'

I squeezed Lizzy's hand gratefully, feeling the warmth of my regard for her, and happy again to be out with my pals to enjoy some music and perhaps even a dance or two.

Inside the hall, the women separated to one side to sit, and sigh, and giggle together, while the men stood around at the other side of the space, smoking cigarettes nervously, and shuffling their feet. The band struck up their first notes and it wasn't long before the bravest of the lads plucked up the courage to ask the girls of their choice for a dance.

Lizzy was the first of us to be asked, of course, then Flora. I sat and watched them, smiling to myself and pleased they were having fun. So when the tall, handsome seaman walked up to me, my smile froze on my face.

'Jesus, I'm not that bad am I?' joked the man, looking deep into my eyes and holding out his hand. 'It would give me the greatest pleasure if you would do me the honour of dancing with me,' he added.

He was well-spoken, and before I could open my mouth to answer, he placed my hand in his and moved towards the dance floor to join the others. I barely had a choice in the matter! He seemed so certain that I had no time to protest, and seconds later found myself looking over the man's shoulder as he gently held my waist and we were moving together to the beat of the music. Throughout the song, he kept up a constant stream of chatter, perhaps sensing my nerves, or perhaps trying to impress me. I said little, except my name.

He told me his name was Joseph, 'but everyone who knows me calls me Jo'. His accent was, to my ears, deep and rather posh, but he had an Irish lilt to it that made me a little giddy. He told me him and his two brothers had been born in Liverpool, but at a young age had moved to Ireland before returning to this city looking for work and better prospects than could be found across the Irish Sea. He said that his brothers had since returned to Ireland, seeing it now as home, but that he had decided to stay.

'I like it here, so I do,' he said with a grin, making his accent markedly Irish as a gentle jest. 'Better looking girls,' he said, giving me a cheeky smile, which made me blush even harder.

With that the tune ended and I turned to go back to my seat, but Jo had other ideas. 'We haven't even started getting to know each other yet. Give me another dance, please Maggie, you'll break my heart so you will if you don't.'

I flushed red again, letting him swirl me into another dance, and another. By the end of the night I felt like I'd been hit by a force of nature. Those bombs and shells had nothing on Jo Clarke. To say he was forceful was an understatement, but he did it in such an alluring way I couldn't help but be charmed by him.

At the end of the evening he told me he was walking me home. I opened my mouth to protest, but Flora chipped in and said we'd all walk together, so clutching my bag, Jo led me from the hall as if we'd been together all along.

Walking home slowly, Jo was the life and soul of the gathering. Flora had met a pleasant looking soldier who was back for a week's leave and already promising undying love, which she did everything to encourage, such was her way. Jo and Flora bantered and laughed as we ambled home. But me, I was daunted by this man who had seemingly forced his way into our evening, and who was already telling anyone who'd listen that he was 'Maggie's man'.

By the time we got to the tenement in Victoria Square that Da, Nellie, Rita and I had recently moved to, Jo had wheedled his way into our group, laughing and joking, all the while holding my hand tightly as if he'd never let me go. The others all clattered off up Scottie Road, leaving me alone with this tall stranger at the entrance to the court surrounded by the towering tenement buildings.

We lived on the fourth floor of one of the blocks, in two squalid rooms that looked down onto the concrete square which was filled with the lines of brick-built air raid shelters. Inside our new home, our rooms felt like they were in constant darkness as the shadows from the buildings drew across our squat space from dawn till dusk. I hated the flat but didn't miss our rooms in Latimer Buildings or Athol Street either, so I supposed that one slum was as good – or as bad – as any other. There were still rats running through the stairwells, lice crawling the walls, and that continual damp stain that leeched through the brick, making the wallpaper hang down in strips.

A fella from the 'corpy', our nickname for Liverpool Council, had been down to inspect some of the homes but we'd heard nothing since. The area had been marked by the Athol Street Redevelopment Scheme of 1938 for demolition, following the Housing Act of 1936. More than 2,000 houses in our small area had been branded 'unfit for human habitation' by the Medical Officer of Health. The corpy didn't need to tell us that! Barely a week went by without one newspaper headline or another shouting about the terrible conditions people were forced to live in. Some areas were largely unchanged from Victorian times and, looking back now, by God the filth of people living on top of each other without proper sanitation was unbelievable. It wasn't so many years earlier that cholera stalked our neighbourhood. But we were poor, and therefore unimportant, and none of us really believed that anything would ever be done to improve our lot.

That night there were a few people about but not many. I suddenly felt unprotected, here alone with this hulking great man, despite the fact he couldn't have been more polite to me.

'You won't go without giving me a kiss, Maggie, I won't let you,' he smiled, but his face was cast in the dim orange beam of the gas light, which gave him a wolfish appearance.

I suddenly felt uncomfortable. I didn't know him, but I also realised that I was no match for his charisma. He was already threatening to overwhelm me, and even though I mistrusted it, there was a small part of me that wanted to feel special again with a man. So I let him give me a quick kiss. Then, with a wink and a tip of his hat, Jo retreated into the night, whistling as he walked. He'd promised to see me tomorrow.

I watched him go, his stride confident, wondering if I'd have any say in the matter over whether Joseph Clarke was for me or not. I sighed, then ran, heels allowing, up those flights of miserable stairs to our rooms where Nellie and Rita were fast asleep. Only Da stayed up, still, waiting for me to return like the kind-hearted soul he was. I lit a single match, the light flaring into the darkness, to set the kettle to boil on the stove, pondering all the while about this new person in my life and wondering why I had such mixed feelings about someone I barely knew.

*

The next day, there he was again, where he'd said he'd be at the time he'd said he'd be there. He was leaning against the tenement wall as I came out to hang the washing on the communal lines strung in higgledy-piggledy fashion. Children screamed past, two boys on a makeshift go-kart, another straggle of boys with a football, yelling and running like wild animals, darting between the shelters and the washing with practiced speed. I saw him and almost dropped my basket of washing.

He loped from his position, covering the length of the square in a few strides. 'It's me, Maggie. How's about I take you out again tonight, would you like that?' he smiled his engaging smile, and his eyes twinkled with merriment.

Was he amused by my obvious discomfort? I decided I shouldn't be so hard on him, after all, he was being a perfect gentleman to me. Even so, my face must have frozen with surprise at seeing him.

'Come on, Maggie, I'm only teasing you! Come out with me tonight, girl, and make me the happiest seaman in Liverpool.'

I gasped at the intimacy of his tone, and before I could stammer an answer, he tipped me a wink and said, 'I'll be here at seven sharp. I'll see you then, Maggie.'

And with that, he walked off, turning once to smile at my bemused face as I stared after him.

When I had finally hung the clothes on the line, rubbed my sore back, and climbed back up the tenement stairs, I sat down at the table in a state of happy shock. He was so good looking, and he wore his clothes so well. Shouldn't I be pleased that such a handsome lad would chase after me?

'Saw you in the court with that sailor,' said Nellie shyly.

She looked pleased. I expect my family had thought I'd given up on men for good!

'He wants to go out with me again tonight, our Nellie, and I don't honestly know what to do,' I replied, looking up at her as she hovered near the bedroom door, a hairbrush in one hand, her prayer book in the other.

'What do ye mean, ye don't know what to do?' she cried, grabbing my roughened hands and smiling into my face. 'When a man like that turns up and wants to go out with ye, ye go, queen. Ye don't ask questions!' Nellie giggled.

She may only have been thirteen years old but she was a mature young woman now with a good head on her shoulders. I pulled my hands away and stroked her lovely face.

'I know, I know. He seems too good to be true though, doesn't he.' It was meant to be a question, but looking back I think it came out as a statement. Perhaps, deep down, I sensed that perhaps he wasn't all he seemed, but his easy-going manner and charm overrode any instincts I had about him then.

'Ye think about things too much, girl. Ye work hard and ye deserve a bit of fun. Ye don't have to marry him. Oh—' with that Nellie had the decency to look shame-faced. 'Sorry, like, I wasn't thinkin'. Ye might still be married . . . Look, if anyone deserves a bit of happiness, our Maggie, it's you. Ye look after us all so why shouldn't someone look after ye for a change. Just go and have a nice time. It doesn't have to be serious.'

I looked up seeing the kindness in Nellie's blue eyes. She meant well. I could see how much she wanted me to be happy, to feel free in some way.

'All right, queen, I'll go out with him.' I patted Nellie's hand and grinned. So that was that.

Nellie looked after Rita who was a bonny girl of almost

three years old, and I got dressed up. At 7 p.m. I looked out of one of the small windows in the main living room. Jo was down there.

'He must've got there early, like,' I said to myself in a quiet voice, knowing that my feelings towards him had softened by seeing him there, alone, waiting for me. With nerves, and a shiver of excitement, I picked up my bag and ran down the stairs, wondering what the night had in store for me.

After that, I saw Joseph every night until he was posted back overseas. He was unfailingly polite, a perfect gentleman to me. Each time I met him he'd produce a small posy of flowers or a little trinket, always some small gift, and I started to treasure them.

Many evenings we'd just walk together, holding hands and talking of our dreams for the future, once this blasted war was over. Joseph was adamant we were meant to be together. One night he turned to me and dropped on to one knee.

'Maggie, you'd make me the happiest man alive if you were to marry me one day,' he said with rather a cheeky grin.

I giggled at that, but he was serious in his own way. We both knew that I may not be free to wed. I'd told Joseph about Thomas McGee and his desertion of me and Rita.

'Get up, Joseph, go 'ed, yer embarrassin' me!' I cried, half-amused by his theatrical gesture, half-touched by the sentiment I knew lay behind it.

'Maggie, darling, I haven't finished yet!' he countered, making me laugh out loud. 'One day, I'll make you my wife, don't you ever forget that,' he finished. His face was deep in shadow, the night dark with the black out. I shivered as he spoke. There was hardly a night breeze, and so perhaps it was a foretelling of our future to come. Whatever it was, I felt uncomfortable for a brief moment, as if my destiny was made by his comments and there was no changing it. I looked down at Joseph's face. He looked sincere. I was just about to open my mouth, to say . . . what? I wasn't sure myself when the air raid siren sounded. Without a second of hesitation, Joseph leapt to his feet, grabbed my hand and we fled to the nearest shelter, stumbling through the dark streets, gripping each other tightly.

We had so little time together due to Joseph's intermittent shore leave, and the time we did have was set against the great conflict raging around us. When we finally crouched next to each other in the shelter, we had no privacy and any questions I had about his idea of our future remained unanswered. When Joseph left for his ship, I felt bereft, as if part of me was missing. Our time together had been so intense, so romantic, and before I knew it, I realised I was head over heels in love with Joseph Clarke.

A great boom rent the air, followed by the *ack-ack-ack* of machine gun fire in the distance. Another explosion seemed to shake the ground beneath our feet. I grabbed Lizzy's hand and together we ran, our hearts in our mouths, towards the rows of brick air raid shelters built into Victoria Square. The air throbbed with the sound of airplane engines, the Luftwaffe in full, raging force. The sky was aglow with burning fires, the cold January evening in 1942 becoming a tornado of brimstone raining down on us.

'Them Germans are on form tonight,' Lizzy shouted above the noise from the deep, pulsing bombers. I gripped her hand tightly as we fled through the dark streets, the searchlights probing the sky, catching the outlines of a dense mass of planes like bees with their humming, and their almighty sting. We reached the shelter and hurried inside. I looked around in the gloom to see whether Da, Nellie and Rita were there but couldn't see them. Me and Lizzy had been out walking, a rare evening where we could talk and catch up with each other's lives, not that anything had changed. I'd left Rita with Da while Nellie put the pan of scouse on to cook. I wasn't too worried. There were three other large shelters in the square especially for our tenements and so they'd have heard the siren go and were, no doubt, hiding in one of the others, though the feeling of being separated from them during a raid nagged at me.

We scrabbled around for somewhere to perch, our breath making icy clouds in front of our faces, most of the makeshift bunkbeds being taken. We found a small section of a wooden bench at one end and sat down together, holding hands for comfort and warmth. The night was bitter. 'So as I was saying,' I continued, the Luftwaffe having interrupted our earlier conversation, 'he wants me to move in with him. I've only known him for seven months but he's so keen. I'm not sure what to do, our Lizzy?'

The nightly raids were expected now, not that they didn't frighten us, but the fear was replaced by a kind of 'live-in-the-moment' feeling. Once we felt safe in the shelter, we could carry on our discussion as if Hitler and his evil armies weren't trying to obliterate us, and our city.

'Our Maggie, I know it's wartime and the usual rules about courting don't apply, queen, but even so . . . ye will be careful won't ye?' Lizzy replied. Even in the dim light I could see she looked concerned.

'But he's found us a place in Old Swan, like, and he says he'll send me money while he's away. I'd have me own kitchen, me own way of doing things, and more than that, I think I love him too,' I replied, searching Lizzy's face for some kind of reassurance from her. I knew things were moving faster than I was completely happy with, but this was wartime, and there was no guarantee any of us would survive so perhaps we should grab happiness when and where we could.

Plenty of young soldiers and seamen had pledged their love to girls they'd known for days or weeks, whereas at least I'd known Jo longer. Joseph had a way of making me see things his way. I could no more stop him from doing what he wanted than I could fly one of those godforsaken bombers. Despite that I'd managed to hold him off by saying we had to wait for a few months to see if we were sure. There'd been no mention of getting married yet, but I assumed that would be the next step.

'But yer'll be living under the brush, Maggie,' stated Lizzy, shaking her head. That was our way of saying that I'd be living in sin, as Jo and I couldn't marry first as to all intents and purposes I was still a married woman, even though I'd had no word from Thomas McGee in almost four years.

'I know,' I sighed, there was no way of getting round that truth. But we were all living under the threat of imminent death, and so it made the matrimonial realities like mine somehow less important. I didn't like the idea of living with Jo without a ring on my finger, but I was sure by now that my husband Thomas had perished overseas, what other explanation could there be for his disappearance? Anyway, I believed it was only a matter of time before Jo popped the question, he was such a gentleman towards me. Yet he was insistent we move in together soon. He'd twist and turn his words, winding me in circles until I didn't know if I was coming or going. It made sense to me at the time to just do as he said and let him worry about the consequences. I was still young, and fancied myself in love with this handsome charmer who'd swept me off my feet.

I'd made up my mind already, if truth be known, and I

just wanted Lizzy to support me and assure me that whatever happened we'd still be friends.

Rat-a-tat-tat! There was a swooning sound of airplanes weaving overhead, swooping like swallows.

'There goes one of ours,' I added. By now we knew the different sounds of the aircraft as they fought over our heads. It was always a good thing to hear some of our boys giving back as good as they got.

'It's a bad one tonight,' replied Lizzy, looking upwards as if she could see through the thick layers of brick and iron above our heads. 'Look, Maggie, ye deserve as much love as this Jo can give ye. Ye have my blessing always, so if it's what you want to do then you must do it. I'll always be there for ye, whatever happens.'

I could barely make out her face in the gloom of the shelter. Lizzy's husband was overseas, my brother Tommy had lost his life at the age of eighteen, this war had claimed too many victims and God only knew whether we were next. At that moment, there was a crash and shudder, and it felt like the earth heaved under us. I squeezed Lizzy's hand gratefully.

'Thanks, queen. Now that one was a bit close out there, I felt it beneath me feet!' We waited, hearing the thunder of the black skies as death and destruction rained down on Liverpool.

When the siren sounded for the all-clear, I stood up, eager to get out of the shelter to find Da, Nellie and my girl Rita. Nothing else really mattered to me, except perhaps the new love that I felt for the charming man who had come to abruptly into my life, and of course my friend Lizzy. We brushed ourselves off with perfunctory brusqueness and prepared to leave relative safety, to carry on with our evening just as if the planes had been part of an ongoing nightmare, phantom lights landing ghostly bombs on our fabled city. Unbeknown to us, it was the last night of bombing Liverpool underwent. The night of 10 January 1942 marked the end of our Blitz, but by no means the end of our war.

CHAPTER 12

Shock Return

27 July 1943 – 1945

The first contraction hit with the force of a tidal wave, the shock of it forcing me to double over, grabbing the tiled wall of the bakery on Latimer Street. It looked like the baby, which wasn't due for another week, had other plans for me than queuing for the day's bread rations. I'd been feeling increasingly insistent twitches and niggles in my tummy for the past day or two, stretching tight across my broad berth, and suddenly they'd transformed into a mighty surge that left me reeling.

'Dear God don't let me waters break in here,' I muttered to myself, feeling breathless with the pain, which was building by the second. My stomach muscles felt like they were squeezing me tight in their iron grip, which of course they were! I'd had enough experience by now to realise that these were no pretend contractions – they were the real thing all right, but how in God's name was I going to get home?

'You all right, queen?' said the kindly bakery assistant, Joanna, who by a stroke of good fortune happened to live close to Victoria Square, where I was living with Da and Nellie while Jo was overseas. I knew her by sight, and by my frequent trips to buy our provisions each day, stepping over rubble and between the carcasses of buildings. Joanna was a young woman in her late twenties, recently married to a docker. She was a pretty girl, and being similar ages we had hit it off straight away.

'Someone help this poor girl here get 'ome, I think the

babby's coming and by the look on her face it won't be long!' cackled the old woman in the queue behind me, who, by the grin on her wizened face, seemed to be rather enjoying the spectacle of someone not far off birthing a child in the shop. Joanna looked flustered. As far as I knew she hadn't yet had children of her own, so the sight of me must have been alarming. Despite this, she shook off her apron and hair net and grabbed my arm.

'Come on, our Maggie, I'll get you home and stay with ye till the midwife gets there,' said my friend, as she carefully guided me through the shop, past the queue of customers, some of whom had the cheek to tut as there was no one else there to serve behind the till. My predicament meant an even longer wait for them than usual!

Slowly, I managed the walk back to Victoria Square at the end of Scottie Road, with Joanna keeping up a stream of chatter all the way, to keep my mind off the baby coming, no doubt. This was my first baby with Jo, but my second child, so I knew what to expect, though I was fearful as any other labouring mother. Our living conditions weren't the best for birthing babies, and it wasn't unusual to hear of women dying in childbirth as the dirt and the squalor caused infection. The babies themselves were also vulnerable. Childhood diseases were rife. Scarlet fever, diphtheria, tuberculosis; they were all too frequent, and I'd been to a few funerals where the coffins were heartbreakingly small, watching mothers like me weep for their newborns. Life was snuffed out so easily it was a wonder any one of us survived, especially as there was a war on. The fragility of our existence always hovered so close, and it was these morbid thoughts that overwhelmed me as the now-familiar contractions reared up inside my body.

Will I survive, dear Lord? Will my child live, Our Lady? I clutched my rosary, drawing strength from the familiar click of the beads as I worried them, praying with the intensity of the labouring mother, that we would both get through the next few hours intact. In those days we needed our prayers, even though we had Walton Hospital on Rice Lane to deliver our babies at.

'Drop me at me Da's,' I said, between exhalations, 'this babby's not long in coming.'

I looked up at Joanna's face, she'd turned paler than I had! 'Go 'ed Maggie, I'm no midwife. You'd better keep yer legs crossed, queen, until I can get ye some help.'

My friend and I staggered up the stairs to Da's flat. When we lumbered in, me breathing in quick, sharp breaths, Joanna holding me under one shoulder with her hand around my expanded waist, Da looked up from his newspaper and let out his form of swear word: 'James's Church!'

Between the two of them, I was gently eased into a chair.

'Just go ring the ozzy will ye and get them to send an ambulance fer me, pleeeeeease.' As I looked to my friend, I was hit by another contraction. They were coming in steady waves now, and I knew we didn't have long to wait.

'Oh God, our Maggie, all right, I'm off. Ye stay there, it'll be all right.' And without another word, Joanna raced off to get help.

She was as good as her word and within a few minutes she was back, rubbing my back and patting my hand in a rather futile attempt to ease my discomfort. By now I was standing up as it made the pains easier to bear. My friend told me a joke she'd heard one of the dockers tell in her shop and I laughed, but then bent over again with the latest surge.

The pains were building. I breathed quickly, punching out my breath, then sighed. I didn't want to give birth on the spot, I wanted a nice, clean hospital for my second baby! The tremors in my body ceased for a couple of blissful minutes, then, 'Ooooooh.'

I could see Joanna's face looking at me in a blur of lipstick and fear but I don't remember much of the next few hours. I made it to Walton Hospital in time, Da at my side. Nellie stayed at home to look after Rita, and I did as all women do, I grunted and groaned my way through a hard, but thankfully short labour, and before I knew it there was a warm bundle in my arms, two unfocused eyes gazing up at me. With a wail, my Eileen had entered the world, and with a contented suckling she softened into it, my second girl.

I cradled my newborn daughter. She was a little beauty, lying in my arms, sated by her first feed. If only her dad could have been there to see her, he'd have been as smitten as I was. With a big yawn, Eileen snuffled and before long was breathing deeply in my arms, having fallen sound asleep, just as if she was saying that the world could wait until she was ready to join it.

In those days we stayed in the maternity ward for ten days to rest and for the baby to get into a routine of feeding and nap times. It was a Godsend having that time away from the chores of daily life, though of course I worried that Rita would miss me. She was now a happy-go-lucky, affectionate little girl of nearly five, who loved music of any kind.

Da, Nellie and Rita came to visit, to see the newest member of our growing family. Despite it being a hot summer day, Da wore his usual 'uniform' of shirt, trousers and braces, his thick docker's jacket and flat cap, which he took off and clutched between his work-roughened hands. He looked out of place in the bright, gleaming hospital ward, with nurses bustling between beds with their strict, no-nonsense way of doing things.

'All right, our Maggie, how are ye, eh?' he asked, approaching my bedside, gazing down at me as I held Eileen up to see her grandfather.

'We're doin' very well, Da. I've got a little girl here who's missed ye, and wants another cuddle'. I held Eileen aloft. It would be the first time her grandda had held her in his arms.

For a second, my father hesitated, looking down at his rough hands. I smiled, realising he felt awkward but wanting him to experience the delight of nestling another granddaughter to his stocky chest, I carefully handed Eileen to him. Da looked uncomfortable at first, but he sat down on the chair next to my bedside, clutching our little baby girl in her bundle of blankets and was soon cooing to her. Nellie and Rita were doing the same, looking at Eileen with wonder in their eyes. They were all utterly taken by her!

I took the chance to close my eyes for a precious few minutes, drifting off into a doze before Eileen's yell woke me.

'She wants her mammy,' chuckled Da, handing her back with reluctance, 'we'll be back to help ye both home in a few days so ye enjoy the rest.' His cap was back on his head, their hospital visit at a natural end.

I beamed back at them, my beloved family here with me, how lucky I was, how blessed we were all able to enjoy this together, only Jo was missing of course.

By the time I took Eileen home, and settled her into her new bed, which was a clean cupboard drawer lined with newspaper and a blanket, we had found our rhythm, our pace feeding and napping together. With Joseph away at sea, things weren't easy. Rita became a good little helpmeet, and would carry the baby, jiggling her when she yelled and hushing her to sleep, as I washed and scrubbed the clouts made of old sheets and cooked up big vegetable scouse to keep us going. The kitchen became a permanently dripping wall of wet and drying nappies, strung on lines nailed into the walls. Lunch was usually a jam butty, smeared with a small amount of butter if we had it, and eaten folded in half.

I felt anguished that Jo was missing out on all this, yet Rita and I seemed to manage. I tried not to notice how well we got on without him, as it meant I might have to notice other things about him that were starting to cause me concern. I was entirely dependent upon him, so I didn't want to acknowledge that feeling, the small seed of an emotion, that spoke gently to me of relief that he was away. After all, he was my man, the father of my Eileen and the love of my life. I'd been happy to be with him, he was the perfect gent, and so I'd even moved in with him before getting married. I'd ignored what society thought of women who lived under the brush.

Yet, something was bothering me. I wasn't perhaps as happy as I'd expected, or feeling as cherished. He was an attractive man and so charming. He was a gentleman to everyone he met; polite, upbeat and full of the blarney. But without meaning to complain, I'd noted that he liked a drink perhaps more than the usual man. I realised quite soon after we settled down together that Friday and Saturday nights were sacrosanct for Jo to be in the alehouses, and sometimes during the week nights as well. Saying that, he always left me a few shillings on the mantelpiece next to the clock for housekeeping so I didn't go short, but then we didn't prosper either.

Of course, Jo was away fighting at sea and now I saw him only on leave. He'd send me money, but when I mentioned it wasn't really enough for the rent, food and upkeep of our lives, he had a way of making me feel like I was asking too much of him, and so I'd end up dropping the subject and hoping that I hadn't upset him. Then by the end of the week, when I was scrabbling about for pennies to pay the butcher, I'd remember that, on his shore leave, he wouldn't spare himself the expense of a few scoops of ale in the evening, or a dapper new trilby hat, or even a pair of new boots, and this made me feel a little sore.

No, there was something not quite right about the way my man left me and Rita with little to spend on essentials, but I racked my brains as to how to raise the subject with him without him getting cross with me. Even thinking those thoughts about him made me feel guilty. After all, he was away risking his life at sea to fight for king and country. I couldn't complain as he sent home bits and bobs of money, enough to get us by. I couldn't ask for more than that, could I? Yet there was always a sinking feeling in my stomach as I eked out the little we had until Jo's next trip home.

I knew there were many worse off than me. We were alive and we had our home, however mean it was, but something nagged at me. Jo had a way of winding me round his little finger, and somehow I always ended up doing exactly what he wanted, but then he was the man of the house and I wasn't in a position to argue!

I was so excited about Jo's next shore leave, that he'd see our baby daughter and be returning to a growing brood, a family of his own. He was only back for a week, and I anticipated his return hourly. I imagined he'd be made up at seeing Eileen for the first time and would be the picture of a doting father.

But on the day he arrived, he was straight in the house, a few shillings put in the usual place, and with a quick peck on the cheek, and a tickle of Eileen's downy soft head, he doffed his smart hat to me and sauntered out of the house down to the local pub. I was gobsmacked.

I stood in the hallway of our place in Old Swan, where I'd returned a few weeks earlier as I now felt able to cope on my own, and stood blinking, unable to gather my thoughts sufficiently to react to what just happened. I couldn't blame him for wanting to stretch his legs and taste the freedom of being home, with his pals and having a time of it, yet there I was, still at home on my own with Rita and our new baby. He'd come home and yet nothing seemed to have changed for me.

I hid my disappointment as best I could, knowing it wouldn't go well for me if I expressed it to Jo. He was sure to tell me that I was overreacting, or not letting him have proper shore leave. Part of me understood that he should enjoy whatever time he had away from the front lines of the still-raging war, but I'd also hoped he'd want to spend some of his time with us, his family.

That first night I sat up waiting for him to come home. I'd missed him, been quite lonely at times on my own, and looked forward to his company. I also wanted to ask him when we'd get married. But when he came in the door, staggering with the drink inside him, in that moment, I saw a different man from the one I'd fallen for. He didn't hit me, as many of the men round here did to their wives after a Friday night spending their wages in the alehouses, but I certainly saw another side to him.

Jo never swore when he was sober, but that night he'd come back cursing and angry at some slight he'd perceived from a drinking pal. They'd had a small flutter on the horses, or the dogs, I forget which, which Jo rarely did, and suddenly my charming, relaxed man was replaced by a bitter, angry drunk. I was so shocked by this transformation that I could barely speak.

'Don't you look at me like that, Maggie. I was cheated I tell you,' Jo raised his voice and stepped towards me. I shrank back into the shadows, the clock ticking, time standing still. Stupidly my first thought was that the neighbours would hear us argue and I felt instantly mortified.

'What? Cat got your tongue has it? Don't you look at me like that, if you didn't spend all my wages I'd still have some in my pocket,' he said meanly, his face a leering mask.

I stepped back, placing my hand protectively against the doorframe, shushing him so that he didn't wake the children.

'Always complaining about money, aren't you? What have you done with my money, eh? Spent it on fancy meat and clothes I'll bet. Jesus, what have I done setting up with the likes of you?' Jo lurched forward, grabbed a chair and sat down heavily, wiping his brow with one hand, silenced at last. He thrust his feet out in front of him and stared gloomily into the glow of the fire embers with his face set into harsh lines. Dark shadows danced softly against the walls.

I turned to pick up his plate with mashed potato and bacon ribs, handing it to him without a word. Jo ate the best out of all of us. If he didn't get meat for his evening meal he'd have a few words to say about it, so often he had the meat and Rita and I ate the leftovers plus the veg and tatties. That's how it was in those days. The man of the house ate the lion's share, and I didn't even think to question it. I knew Jo didn't mean what he was saying, but even so his words stung.

I realised it was only because he had been drinking that he'd become like this, grouchy and critical. It made such a contrast to his hard-working days, where he'd greet me with a kiss each morning and be up and ready to provide for his family at the crack of dawn. With a grunt he began devouring the meal, and I had a few moments to sit and watch him as he ate. There was stubble on his chin and a cold glint in his eyes, but he looked like the same Jo I'd fallen in love with.

I sighed, not understanding what had just passed between

us, but with a realisation dawning that life wasn't going to be as easy or as simple as Jo had promised. But then, who was life easy or simple for?

The rest of the week was also difficult. Jo was out seeing his pals each night, leaving me alone with Rita and the baby. He seemed to hardly notice us and that saddened me. I tried to keep a smile on my face and be understanding. How could I possibly know what it was to be a man in these dreadful times, having to go to war, risking life and limb every second of each day. I supposed he needed to blow off steam on his homecomings, but there was a part of me that wanted my polite, loving man back, just for an hour, so we could be happy and I could feel we were together as a proper couple.

Things were also hard with him and Rita. He seemed to resent her presence as she wasn't his own daughter. By the end of the week, Jo's money had gone, and he'd even taken out shillings from my housekeeping. When he doffed his hat to me, kissed my cheek and threw his bag jauntily over his shoulder, walking away from us with a whistle, I felt a sigh of relief escape my lips. I shut the front door and my face hardened. Something wasn't right, but there was nothing at all I could do about it. I had to carry on with life and hope that Jo would come to his senses after this war and realise what a loving family he had.

The weeks following his departure were terrible. There was no money and I was forced to go 'on the parish' which meant going on the dole in those days. There was little else I could do, and I was grateful that me and my children wouldn't starve, after all the Great Depression of the 1930s that affected us all was only a decade away. Despite that, I was ashamed to sink so low, and in my heart I blamed Jo. I couldn't work, I had a new baby and Rita to care for, and few other options. Each night I prayed for the war to end, for Jo to come home to us a changed man and for the safety of my family. I prayed the way I had with my mammy.

Back then, I'd put my head on her knee and she'd intone, 'God bless Daddy. God bless Mammy. God bless Maggie, and Tommy and Nellie'. Now it was my turn to sit, with Rita's head against my leg, stroking her dark hair and saying: 'God bless Grandda, God bless, Jo. God bless Da. God bless Rita, and Eileen, and even, God bless me and keep us safe, keep us together'.

It was two years later, almost two months after VE Day when the streets of Liverpool had thronged with people of all ages celebrating the end of war in Europe. I was returning home from queuing for the day's rations, I opened the front door to find a letter on the mat. I picked it up, wondering who would write to me. I knew it wasn't an official letter from the War Office as they were always brown envelopes and this was a small, plain white one with handwriting I half-recognised. Frowning, I set my basket down, hurried Rita inside and carried Eileen, thinking to make a cup of tea and sit down to read it. I set the kettle to boil but curiosity got the better of me.

I opened the missive carefully and began to read. It was from Thomas McGee.

CHAPTER 13

Divorce

1945

There was a single, hard, knock at the door. I jumped, though I had been expecting the sound. Putting down my tea cup, it rattled as it touched the saucer, showing how nervous I was at this encounter. It was several days since receiving that letter from my husband, Thomas McGee, and I felt like I'd been assailed by every single kind of emotion within those hours.

When I'd first opened the letter, I scanned the few lines, rereading to make sure I had taken it in properly, before letting it slip from my fingers and fall to the ground. I'd sat down, heart thumping, my palms sweating, with a desire to wail overcoming me. He was alive. Thomas was back in Liverpool on leave from the army, and he wanted to see his daughter.

Why hadn't I heard anything from him since he'd left, the morning after we were wed? I thought I'd laid that hurt and that disappointment to rest, but his sudden reappearance in my life had made me a liar to myself. I was deeply unsettled, dreading the sight of him yet craving an explanation for his disappearance, which still felt so cruel to me and our child.

I wanted to know why he'd not written to us, why he hadn't replied to any of my letters and the photograph I'd sent him of our Rita. To me, who valued family above all else in life, I simply couldn't understand how someone could walk away without a word or a gesture, leaving us to guess and speculate, and never knowing the truth. I'd also mourned him as dead, killed in battle perhaps. I made myself believe that he was

164

missing in action and that was why I never heard anything from the War Office. But that wasn't the case. Thomas, my Thomas as he had been, had simply decided to forget us, to leave and not look back, and I still felt the deep pull of that wounding over my first love.

I put my hand to my stomach to try and quell the fluttering of panic and fear. That was him. I hadn't seen Thomas since the morning after we married, seven long years ago, and he was now standing at my door.

I looked over at Rita who was absorbed in playing with her doll, chattering away to herself as she cared for it. How would Rita react to seeing the father she'd never known, who'd abandoned her, to all intents and purposes? I stood up, taking all my courage in my heart to do it, and smoothed down my apron. Checking my glossy hair in the mirror by the front door, I stepped forward to meet the man who had remained a mystery until today.

I could barely breathe as I opened the door. Thomas was standing there, straight and tall in his army uniform. I inhaled, he still had the power to make me swoon a little, but my hurt feelings held that off. I wanted answers from him. I was no young girl of seventeen any more, as I was when he first kissed me, I was a full grown woman of twenty-five with two children. I realised in that moment I was made of sterner, stronger stuff, and I could face him at long last.

Thomas stared back at me, his eyes flinty, cold-looking. He was bronzed brown by the overseas sun, and his face had lines where there were once smooth contours. He still looked handsome, but my heart shrank from him, from this man who had caused me so much upset.

'Come in,' I said woodenly, gesturing for him to enter. He said nothing but followed me down the corridor and into my small but bright kitchen area. Still nothing was said between us. He stood, waiting, and I turned to put the kettle on but his voice stopped me.

'I don't want tea, Maggie, I just want to see me daughter,' was all he said. He took off his cap and placed it on the table. I watched as a small cloud of dust particles rose into the beam of sunlight crisscrossing the table.

'Why didn't ye write to me, Thomas,' I whispered, my voice cracked with emotion. It didn't matter what the answer was, I could cope with anything he might say to me, but I wanted to know for my own peace of mind.

There was silence. Thomas looked away from me, his gaze scanning the small room with its dishrags out for drying, the pile of nappies on the side cabinet and my few dishes and pans on the shelf above the cooker.

'I want to see me daughter,' was his reply.

I felt a sudden rise of bile in my throat. I wanted answers. He'd left us alone and unprotected. I deserved to know. 'Tell me, Thomas!' I almost choked on my suppressed hurt.

This time he looked back at me and his eyes weren't kind, not like they were when we were courting. 'I told yer, Maggie, I want to see Rita, where is she?'

There was a noise from the doorway and our daughter stood there, a shy six-year-old girl, with her best frock on so that her daddy wouldn't have anything to complain about how I was bringing her up. I swallowed down my emotions so that Rita wouldn't see how much this exchange was costing me. I didn't want her to pick up on the bad feeling there seemed to be between us.

'This is yer daddy, Rita. Do ye remember what I said about him visitin' us today, like? He's come here to say hello because he wants to see ye very much. Do you think ye can say hello to him, angel?' I kept my voice deliberately calm and bland, all the better to see Thomas's reaction.

Rita was a gorgeous little girl, with her father's dark hair and my blue eyes. She looked at Thomas from the corner of her eye, then ran over to me, gripping my legs and staring back at him. Who could blame her? It was the first time she'd ever set eyes on the man who fathered her. He was a complete stranger to her – to us both now – and she clearly didn't understand why he was here. I couldn't blame her for that either.

'Say hello to yer daddy, me darling, then ye can go off and play. Yer dinner'll be ready in half an hour. Go on, girl, just a hello, please.'

My voice was pleading now. I don't know why I wanted our daughter to give a good account of herself, but I did. I didn't want Thomas saying I couldn't bring up our daughter properly, though his good opinion should not have mattered to me.

The moment had been broken by Rita's appearance. I couldn't find the space to keep asking him why he'd abandoned us. Instead, I half-wailed, 'We thought ye were dead.' Shaking my head, I felt tears come, hot and fast.

'Well, I can see that, Maggie. Yer livin' with someone else even though yer me wife before God and the law. And yer've had another baby.' He spat the words out, his anger at the situation clear to see.

My Jo's reaction to me receiving the letter from the man who was still my husband had been so different, so unexpected. If anything, he'd played it down, dismissing my fears and telling me I was overreacting. How could I be overreacting? The man I'd presumed dead for many years had walked into my home as if back from the dead.

We both looked over at Eileen, who was playing quietly with her doll on the floor.

'So what if I have, Thomas McGee?' I retorted. 'We

thought you'd been killed. We heard nothing from you in seven years. Seven years!' My feelings rose in me. I wanted to hit out at him, show him what his actions had cost me. He'd broken my heart, I wasn't going to let him off quite so easily, but at that moment I suddenly felt desperately sad. I'd loved Thomas in my own way, and he'd let me down, and now here we were, arguing in my kitchen, while our daughter looked at him like he was an alien from another planet.

Thomas crouched down to try to coax Rita to him but she clung tight to my legs still, resisting his attempts to speak to her. With a sigh he got back up and we stood together, both awkward,.

'Maggie, I want a divorce,' is all he said.

The room was filled with those words, they were so powerful. I heard them and something inside me collapsed. Whatever anger I felt at Thomas dissolved into a bloom of sadness for us both that things didn't work out the way we'd planned during our courtship. We'd married, had a baby and yet here we both were, with years' worth of unanswered questions, and fresh hurts on top. Perhaps it was best this way. A clean break, us both free to carry on with our lives.

I nodded. What else could I do? I'd borne another man's child while I was still married to him. I'd moved in with Jo and started a new life. It wasn't an easy life but it was my choice and I was building a new family as best I could.

Divorce was a word that sat uncomfortably with us. It went against our faith, our religion and creed, but it was the only real option ahead of us. I nodded again. It was over. Whatever had taken place between Thomas and myself was finally done. I would probably never get an answer from him, and I would never know why that was. Bemused and unhappy, I showed him out of the door, shutting it and leaning my forehead onto the cool wood. I stayed there for a while, until

Eileen, who was nearly two years old, and Rita squawked for my attention, both trying to grab the same doll and fighting like the small children they were.

I allowed myself a smile at last. It had been a rough morning, but things moved onwards, they always did. And now it was time for me to get the dinner on the table, as if nothing at all had happened. I'd already got the stock nice and hot, and had peeled a few carrots, potatoes and leeks, and today I had the leftover bones from yesterday's scrag end of lamb to add to the pot. I had some fresh herbs from the Scottie Road market and I added them, stirring and smelling the thick, brown liquid.

There was nothing like a pan of scouse to lift my spirits. In the midst of all the confusion and trouble life sometimes threw at us, it was something heartening. It was a simple meal, but it said everything to me about keeping home and hearth together. It was a family meal, and one I'd cooked a million times over for my father, Tommy and Nellie. I carried on stirring, thinking of Tommy's cheeky face as a boy, his legs swinging off the one chair we owned as he was too small for them to touch the ground, and I heard again the shrieks of delight as I spooned out quantities of home-made stew.

The smell reminded me of those days just after Mam left us, when Da would come in, tired from work and heartbroken from his wife's desertion, and I'd ladle out his dinner. He'd always sigh a small sigh of relief, to be home, safe and well, and with food on the table. Our ritual was always the same. Dish out the scouse, settle down at our seats and stop talking, then hands together for Da to say grace. We'd chorus 'Amen', cross ourselves, each blessing our dinner in our own way, then we'd launch into our meal, devouring the good, thick, hot stew that would keep our bellies full for another day. Tommy would chatter about school or about playing football with the lads in the court, and how they'd broken one of old Father O'Rourke's collection of glass bottles, and how they'd be sent on errands for a ha'penny. Nellie would join in, laughing and giggling, telling us in her babyish high voice about the rats in the yard and how one of the boys in the street had chopped a tail off and they'd run away, screaming with terror and more than a little childish excitement.

We had nothing but we had each other, and the pan of stew on the range was the central focus for our family evenings together. I needed that feeling back today, a salve for my long-held emotional wounds. Thomas's visit had upset me, even though there was at least now a sense of finality. No more could I wonder and pray for him. He'd chosen to leave us, for whatever reason, and I had to get on with my life for Rita and Eileen's sake.

I watched the pot bubble away, set the table then called out to the children to be seated. It was in my power to give them those same happy family memories; a pan of scouse and full bellies. The stew would last for days, topping it up with lentils, onions and barley to make 'peawhack', as we called it. I smiled to myself as I ladled out the meal and felt the contentment of a mother seeing her babies eat that day. Never again would I think about why Thomas left. It was over. Life had to go on, and what better way than with a plate of good, homemade stew.

I didn't have time to mull over the events with Thomas McGee. I'd popped over to Victoria Square to check in on Da and Nellie, see they were feeding themselves properly and check the place was as clean as it was possible to make it, and instead I found my seventeen-year-old sister sat at the kitchen table in tears. 'Y'all right, our Nellie, what's the matter, girl? Someone gone and broken yer heart!' I joked, taking off my hat and overcoat as Eileen skipped through the door in front of me. Rita was at school so I'd taken the opportunity to travel over.

One look at Nellie's stricken face and I realised I'd hit the nail firmly on the head. Cursing inwardly for my lack of sensitivity, I went straight over to Nellie and put my arm round her shoulder. 'Oh luv, what is it? Come on, queen, tell me and I'll see if I can't make it better. Things can't be that bad, eh?' My voice was lost in the spasm of crying that hit Nellie, and so I scooped her into an embrace, feeling her body jerk against me until her emotions were spent.

I smoothed back her hair, whispering that it would all be all right, when she said, 'Our Maggie, ye don't know what I've done. I've gone and got meself in the family way.'

'Ah,' I replied, exhaling a long breath. 'And who's the father, like? Does he know and will he do the right thing by ye?'

My voice was steady, but I instinctively felt panic rise in me. Girls left with a baby and no husband were looked down upon I'd faced that prospect myself and I knew how that felt, and I didn't want Nellie to have to battle that every day of her young life, as well as bring up a child alone. I held my breath, waiting for her response.

'It's me fella Walter, I've been seeing him fer a while . . .' Her voice trailed off. I'd known she was being courted by a young man called Walter Horrocks; as I've said before, there wasn't much around our way that stays a secret for long. He lived with his mother in Scotland Road, not far from Nellie, and they'd met at a picture house and started courting while he was on shore leave. The rest, as they say, was now history.

'I went over to see Walter to tell him the news but he weren't there and I saw his mammy instead,' Nellie sobbed, 'and she guessed of course, and offered me ten shillings to "forget all about it". I think she meant to get it seen to by one of the women who helps girls in trouble, or she might've meant that I go off and not tell Walter he's going to be a daddy. I don't know what she meant but I ran from there and told him anyway, like. He has a right to know.' Nellie looked fierce at that point, and it was then I saw how much she had her mam Mary's fire within her. Nellie, of all us kids, looked most like Mammy, and she sang as well, if not better, than Mary did. She wasn't singing now.

Her tearstained face crumpled again as the fight left her. 'What am I goin' to do?' she said as she burst into fresh tears.

'Well, our Nellie, first things first. I'm goin' to put the kettle on and make a cuppa. And then, we're going to work out how we tell Da. He'll expect Walter to marry ye, ye know that don't yer?' I said, as I got up and started organising the tea things, feeling calmer now I was doing something practical.

'He said he'll marry me, he's promised, like,' sniffed Nellie, rubbing her red eyes, making them look even more sore.

Nellie was a young woman with her whole life ahead of her, but now she'd got herself pregnant, and there was nothing we could do about it except get her married to Walter as fast as humanly possible. Walter Horrocks was a seaman in the Merchant Navy, as so many lads around here by the docks were. He was a nice enough lad, perhaps a little wayward, but if Nellie was right and he'd promised to marry her then there was nothing at all to worry about. Even if he didn't do the right thing, then I knew that Da, as head of our family, would welcome the newest Riley family member with open arms. After all, he'd stuck by me.

'I'm scared of havin' a baby, our Maggie. Does it hurt much?' Nellie looked so young as she turned to ask me that.

Not wanting to frighten her, I shushed her like a child,

and poured steaming hot tea into her cup. 'Drink up, we've got some big news to tell our father, and we'd better decide when we'll break it to him,'

Later that evening, Nellie calmly told Da her news. He was as kind as he'd been to me, holding her in his arms and telling her he couldn't wait to be a granddad again. Not for the first time, I said a grateful prayer, thanking God for giving us such a kind, loving man as a father.

By the time Nellie gave birth to her son Tommy at the end of November 1945, there was more than a new baby to be happy about. Tommy was born in a time of peace. The Second World War had finally ended on 2 September 1945. There was an outpouring of joy, as Liverpudlians joined the nation in celebrating, with the pubs staying open all day, drinking and dancing in the streets and street parties for the children. Nellie and Walter were made up with their son. They quickly announced their wedding date on 15 February 1946. The shadow of war had lifted, and although there was sadness as the human cost of the war was remembered and honoured, peacetime had come at last. Life finally seemed to be moving forward for all of us.

CHAPTER 14

Joseph Returns

1947–49

There was a stumble, an uncoordinated movement. Then, the sound of a fist pounding the door. 'Let me in, Maggie, I can't find my key.'

I waited a moment, wondering what would happen if I ever found the courage to bar that door to keep him out. It was long past 11 p.m. on a chilly autumn night, and Jo had been in the pub since five o'clock. It was a Friday, the night that most workers took the opportunity to sink a few beers and wipe away the week's labours. A time to have a few laughs then head home for their dinner, buoyed up by their companionship and shared troubles. Not for Jo, though. His drinking bouts seemed to have worsened steadily. He'd always spent each Friday and Saturday night in the pub and these days were no different, but there was no way of denying it to myself any longer – he was a drunk. He had tipped into the kind of drunk that staggered back to the wife he'd left at home, and the children he'd neglected, and Our Lady herself would've turned away from him, or so I thought.

I bit my tongue on his return, knowing that it would be worse for me if I said a word against him. But, I watched, I saw how he was spending our money on his pals and the drink they all relished. In my eyes, he squandered the wages he earned as a crane driver, leaving me, Rita and Eileen with only just enough to feed us and keep a roof over our heads. I was no saint; if truth be known, I resented him for that. But when I heard him shuffling up the steps, banging at our door, like tonight, I shuddered and shrank back, hoping against hope he wouldn't take his sodden anger out on me.

'What are you doing in there, Maggie Clarke, let me in my own house. So help me God, it's cold as ice out here.' His voice was slurred but his venom was crystal clear.

'I'm comin' Jo, no need to wake the whole Old Swan tennie up,' I replied at last, worrying that everyone in the tenement would hear. Unlocking the door, I got out of his way, fast, once he was inside the threshold. I looked him up and down from the corner of my eye. His blue eyes were bloodshot, his blond hair slick with sweat, yet he still carried himself like a prince, despite the fact he was a thirty-three-year-old man who was more than half-cut on ale.

'I'm ready for my dinner, now, and I don't want none of that scouse you made earlier, I want proper meat for my tea.' He turned to me, his face ugly with drink.

I stammered. There was nothing else. His housekeeping money, placed on the mantelpiece every Friday before he got changed into his dapper new clothes and left for the ale-house, had not been enough to buy decent meat this week as Eileen, who was a growing girl of four, had needed shoes. I tried to explain this to him, but my words were greeted by a dense silence and I knew trouble was on its way.

'You're telling me that there's no decent meat in my dinner again? You're tellin' me that the money I put into your pocket to feed us is not enough? What have you spent the house-keeping on then?' he leered. His voice was low, menacing.

Jo was paid eight pounds, six shillings a week – a good wage at the time. He gave me half of that for housekeep-ing, but that four pounds had to pay our weekly rent of ten shillings and sixpence, as well as all our food and clothing, coal and rations. It was useless trying to explain to Jo that rationing had been restricted further, down to one shilling's worth of meat per week. He wouldn't listen, and if he did, he'd have wanted that butcher's portion all for himself. But he worked hard, and he put food on the table, so I couldn't complain. He wasn't a bad man as such, it was just that the drink changed him, made him mean, and for that I couldn't completely forgive him.

'Jo, I'm doin' the best I can with the money ye give me, like. It's hard to get anythin' but scraps of meat from the butcher these days. I queue for hours every day fer potatoes or mouldy old veg. It's not like it used to be. This war has left us all in the mire, so please don't go blamin' me, our Jo,' I countered, feeling suddenly weary to my bones. I wanted to tell him that if he didn't drink away his wages, if he didn't spend lavishly (to my eyes) on new clothes for himself – shiny boots, a new trilby hat, a good suit and ties – then we'd eat a lot better. But I didn't dare. Jo would go mad, and I didn't want him waking the girls and adding to their miseries.

'Anyway, Jo, yer didn't give me anything last week, re-member. I've been eking out what we have, but I can't buy anythin' with thin air.' I was amazed to hear the strength in my voice, though inside I was shaking. I wasn't lying. What I was saying was true, but even so, I trembled to think what Jo would say back to me.

Predictably he didn't take it well. 'Don't you go blaming me, Maggie, if you spend all the money I give you. Jesus Christ. All I want is to grab a bite after a hard week's work and this is what I get. Nagged from dawn till dusk. It's time you gave me some respect, Maggie, or I'll never give you an-other penny again.' With that, Jo slumped into a chair and took off his trilby, settling it as carefully as he was able, given his state, on the table. He glared at me as I ladled the day's stew, cutting him a slice of the disgusting brown bread that was all we could get at the bakery.

Us housewives resented rationing after the privations of the war. We'd scrimped and saved all our lives, and then hoped for better times once the war was won and our boys were home. Yet, despite our victory, Liverpool, and Britain I supposed, felt a bleaker place. Everything was rationed; meat, butter, lard, sugar, clothing, soap, and now even potatoes were restricted, though we were betting that the Princess Elizabeth's forthcoming November marriage to Prince Phillip wouldn't involve scrimping with ration coupons! There were rumours that her wedding cake would be as high as the ceiling, and she'd be wearing a full-length lace gown. The wedding had been the centre of our gossip for months since the engagement in July, though some felt the extravagance was out of place when so many of us were living with real privations. I didn't mind. I liked to see the young queen-in-waiting marry her Prince Charming. I felt it gave the nation a boost, though I wouldn't be going down to London to bed down outside Buckingham Palace for the days prior to the ceremony like so many others across the nation!

Princess Elizabeth wasn't the only one who wore good clothes. My Jo paid proper money for his fancy knock-off black market clothing, while me and the kids wore utility clothes, which were poorly made and drab. I had managed to get sausages the other week after queuing for two hours, but they were bland tasting and, anyway, I'd got them for Jo's dinner so that he felt well fed. The price of coal had rocketed to almost five shillings a bag, and so I only ever had a fire going in the kitchen as the evenings drew in. On top of that, the winter was coming and everyone seemed to be predicting it would be a bad one this year with snow storms and ice. I shivered just thinking about it. Could things possibly get worse? I guess I should've known the answer to that.

'Here's yer dinner, it's stew. I do me best, Jo, I promise you,' I offered gently, holding the plate out to him.

For a moment, for an inkling of a moment, I thought he might throw it back at me. He didn't. He just grunted and, picking up a spoon, started to shovel it into his mouth. Once he was finished, he shoved the plate towards me, and wordlessly I picked it up and took it to the scullery to rinse.

This was our life. Me waiting in for him to come home, stinking of cheap ale and perfume from the alehouses, while I counted the pennies and did what I could to keep us going. I sighed. I knew many women had it worse than me. Many men didn't come home from the war, and so their wives and families found themselves thrown into poverty or living back with in-laws. At least I had Jo here, and whatever I thought about him on nights like this, that were all too frequent, he paid the rent and fed us. He might have had more than his fair share of Irish charm as well, but to my knowledge he'd never cheated on me neither. He wasn't a ladies' man, despite his good looks and swagger. In some ways, I was lucky. I just had to keep remembering that.

'I'm off to my bed.' Jo wiped his face on the dishrag and threw it to the floor before getting up slowly, and with a sloping gait, disappeared into the bedroom.

We were lucky enough to have two rooms for sleeping in, so Eileen and Rita shared one, and Jo and I the other. I looked at the dark, empty doorway he'd passed through then bent down to pick up the cloth, placing it back in the scullery and turning off the light before joining him. He was already snoring when I crept into bed. I turned on my side and a single tear rolled down the side of my face, blooming into the fabric of the pillow.

*

Pushing aside the curtain, I crouched inside the confessional box, making the sign of the cross and intoning, 'In the name of the Father, and of the Son and of the Holy Spirit. My last confession was six days ago . . .' I drew in a breath as the dark shape of the priest shifted. Squeezing my eyes shut, I began to speak the familiar words: 'Forgive me, Father, for I have sinned . . .' I listed my misdemeanours as I saw them, leaving my problems with my relationship until I'd exhausted all other confessions.

I admitted to a sharp word with a neighbour, and to feeling envy for someone better off than us, and when I finished those I took in a deep breath and told the priest what was really troubling me. 'Forgive me, Father, but I feel so much anger towards my Jo at the minute. So much anger. I hate feeling like this.

'He's not bad, as such. He works and he pays the rent, and gives me housekeeping, but I hate him going out to the pubs, like. It's just that I want him home with me so that we can have family time together. Since he's been back from the war he's been different to the man I met.'

I stopped for a moment. My story must be a familiar one, as men and women adjusted to their lives together after wartime. How many women lamented the changes in their husband's spirits and personalities after they faced the brutalities of war? I knew I wasn't alone in experiencing this, but that didn't mean I didn't feel lost, and somehow cheated by the war as a result. Jo's drinking had increased since the war, and his manner with me was cold, hostile even. He never shouted but he sneered, belittled me. I wanted to sympathise, to ask him what he'd seen in active service, the horrors he must've encountered, but Joseph Clarke was as closed to me as the priest behind the wooden grille that separated us.

The priest remained silent, his profile a shadow.

'I love him, I do love him, like.' I wondered if I was trying to convince myself, and sighed again, 'it's just that I don't recognise him sometimes. He used to be so attentive, so different towards me. Sometimes I feel like we're worlds apart . . .'

It was no good. Despite the relief I felt at unburdening myself before God in the form of His messenger, my local priest, this time I couldn't shake the feeling that it wasn't my fault, and I was right to feel the frustration I did. I didn't feel truly sorry for my sin of anger, and so I wasn't following the teachings of my faith. Tears threatened, and I didn't trust myself to say anything further.

The priest, sensing my reluctance, gave me my penance; three Hail Marys and four Our Fathers, and I was also told to spend time in prayer for Jo and to thank God for the gift of His mercy.

I stayed in the church most of that morning, on my knees before the altar, being with the presence that had comforted me for most of my life. I came away, if not happier, then at least a little calmer. I prayed to God for my man, to help him stop his drinking, and that was all I could do. The rest was up to God, and Jo himself. Even though I knew that nothing could make Jo want to be a family man, I still felt more hopeful, as if I wasn't completely powerless over the situation, and all because of a few whispered heartfelt prayers.

Walking home, I bumped into my school friend Mary Livingstone, who now lived just a few streets away from me in Old Swan. My worries must have been written all over my face, despite the time I'd spent praying, because Livy, who was a slim woman of about the same height as me, with brown hair and a sweet smile, instantly looked concerned.

'Where have those worry lines come from, eh queen?' She made an attempt to cheer me up straight away.

I opened my mouth to make a joke of it, but to my horror I burst into unhappy tears instead!

'Our Maggie, what's wrong, queen, ye look like you've got the troubles of the world on yer shoulders!' she exclaimed. Mary looked me up and down, before grabbing hold of my arm and steering me in the direction of my flat. 'There's nothing in this world that a natter and a cuppa can't solve, queen. Now, come on, let's go 'ome and have a nice chat. Yer probably just tired, eh, all those kiddies to look after, and that Jo, well he's enough to test the patience of a saint.'

As she said that, I burst into fresh tears. Everyone knew our troubles, or guessed at them, and all of a sudden I felt as weak as a newborn lamb.

'Oh dear, we'd better make it a strong brew hadn't we luvvie, with plenty of sugar if you've got it, girl,' smiled Mary as she bundled me up the stairs.

We reached my front door, and I rattled my keys from my bag. We stepped inside. I was relieved to see that I'd left the kitchen spick and span before going out this morning. Dumping my basket on the kitchen table, I turned to Mary, unpinned my hat, and spoke at last.

'Don't mind me, I'm not meself today, that's all it is, our Mary. It was good of you to see me home, like, but I don't need any help. Everythin's fine, I've nothing to complain of.'

I tried a weak smile that clearly didn't fool my pal. We'd known each other since we sat together in the classroom at St Sylvester's so not much got past either of us where our friendship was concerned. 'Course you haven't, our Maggie, now where's the tea leaves, I'll set the kettle to boil, then we'll set the world to rights.'

I sat down in my own kitchen and looked at Mary as she bustled to the cooker to set the enamel kettle to boil. Clinking the tea cups and saucers, she poured boiling water onto the loose tea leaves in the teapot and poured out the milk. *I could've had Mary's life if it wasn't fer the drink*, I thought to myself.

Mary had moved to Old Swan with her husband Ted. They had a daughter Rose who was friends with my Eileen. Mary was the very epitome of a happily married woman, content with her lot in life, and a happy home with enough money to get by without squabbles. I envied her then, I guess, even though we'd been friends for so long and wouldn't wish anything but good to her and her family.

'You timed it well, Mary, I managed to get some milk yesterday. Had to queue for nearly an hour, mind. It's a blinkin' lot of waiting around to get even the basics these days. Ye'd have thought that winning the war would've solved all our problems eh . . .?' I smiled but my chin wobbled.

Mary passed me my tea. 'No biscuits I'm afraid, no sugar neither,' I smiled again. We didn't have the money for Rich Teas or Garibaldis, and I couldn't find sugar in the local shops for love nor money.

'No problem, our Maggie,' was all she said, stirring her cup and looking over at me.

'Sorry to cry like that, things have got on top of me a bit, being silly really . . .' I coughed. I didn't need to say any more than that, Jo's drinking was hardly a secret and it was pointless moaning as there was nothing on God's earth I could do about it. It felt good to have the companionship though. It made things seem a little brighter.

I had a pile of washing folded up on the cabinet, ready to hang out to catch the last of the autumn sunshine, then the front steps needed scrubbing and the floors were looking dusty again. For once, I decided to put off my chores and sip the scalding hot tea. A small shaft of sunlight lit the table top, and the dust particles rose up like a flower shedding its seeds.

Mary spoke first, 'The way I see it is this, queen, there's nothing you can do about your Jo and his ways, though you don't like them. The men, they don't listen to us. So the best you can do is put up with it, and not give him cause to give you more aggravation.'

I sighed. 'Life isn't easy, like, it's not easy.'

Mary nodded.

We both sat, sipping the hot liquid, musing on both of our destinies. Had we imagined that life would be any different? As young girls, what did we dream our future would be? For a moment I was transported back to Mary's and my First Holy Communion at the age of seven. It was a big occasion, and even my mam did her bit, making a white dress for me, out of goodness knows what fabric. How she got hold of it I'll never know. She made me a short veil, and the dress with flounces that ended just below my knees, making me feel like a proper princess. It was so special.

Mary Livingstone, Lizzy Murray and me, along with our classmates, were all dressed like little brides, and some even carried a small posy. We walked together through our streets, down Scottie Road to St Anthony's Church. The priest gave me a medal with a picture of Our Lady's face on it and a prayer book, which I clutched with the passion of a young girl transported by the ritual. The ceremony, so beloved by our community, marked our passage from babies to young people, growing up within spiritual parameters as well as physical ones. I remember the feeling of belonging, of being part of something bigger than myself, and a sense that the future was somehow secure and blessed by God.

Looking across the table now at Mary, I couldn't help but wonder where that clarity, where that optimism, had gone from my life. I'd made my bed and by God I was now lying in it, though sometimes it chafed my soul to do so. After all, what else could I do? I had no money of my own, nowhere to go if times got tough. I just had to carry on and deal with each day as it came, and try to find the small points of joy within those days.

At that moment Rita ran in, back from school. She was nine years old and a happy girl, except for the moment that Jo stepped into the house. Then, she was wary, quiet, always expecting a lashing from his tongue or a spiteful comment from him. Jo had no love for Rita, and he showed it in many carelessly cruel ways. He'd shout at her, he'd moan about earning money to feed her, and woe betide me if I tried to buy my daughter a new coat or shoes, he'd really have something to say about that. Despite his gruff protestations, he never once stopped me getting what she needed, but I saw the pain he gave my little girl and I kept her close whenever Jo was in the house. He was never like that to four-year-old Eileen. I expect that was because she was his by blood, though I could hardly call him a good father, he was too wedded to his ale for that. It upset me more than I would admit to see him treat Rita so differently to his own daughter.

'All right, our Rita, hungry? How was school?' I sang as she skipped towards me, her lovely face lit up with pleasure at being home and finding just me and my friend here. Eileen followed in behind her. She was so tiny, barely old enough to be out at school, but her face was also a picture of that excitement all young children feel at hearing the school bell for the end of the day. Both their knees were scuffed from playing in the street, and their hands and faces were dirty. They looked like real ragamuffins!

'Mam! It was a good day but I'm starving!' she said, as she wrapped her arms around me and gave me a kiss.

'Now then, if you'll let me up, I can do you a jam butty each, would ye both like that?' I laughed, pretending to disentangle myself from her skinny arms. Neither of my girls was chubby, we ate too sparingly for that, but they were both bright as buttons and happy as much as they could be, in light of the shadow Jo cast over us.

The girls squealed their delight at the thought of their favourite sandwich.

With a burst of happiness, I got up and pulled on my apron. 'Time for me to get goin',' said Mary, sensing our chat had come to a natural end, and pulling her coat back on.

'Thanks, queen,' I said, giving her a nod, the kind of gesture that women show to each other as a way of understanding, of mutual comprehension. The arrival of my girls had lifted the gloom. I wondered if God had answered my prayers today by taking my mind off my troubles; a friend and two beautiful children to care for. Suddenly I felt a sense of the awe of my religion, my understanding of divinity, and it helped me move towards the rest of my day, cleaning, cooking, scrubbing and dinner on the table in time for Jo's return in an hour. Suddenly my life didn't seem all that bad.

Nearly two years later, in 1949, I realised I was expecting another child. It was six years since Eileen was born, and I'd assumed that God and Mother Nature had forgotten me when it came to babies. How wrong I was. When I told Jo we were having another babby to add to our brood, he did what Jo did best; gave me a wink and a smile, grabbed his wallet and headed out to the local pubs to celebrate.

I watched him go, whistling as he went, his suit looking as smart as anything I'd seen in the magazines. He was still an attractive man. I was twenty-nine years old and Jo was five years older than me, but he looked dapper. I knew it was the tradition for the men to celebrate by buying their pals yet more rounds in the alehouses, but, not for the first time,

I wished fervently he'd celebrate at home with me, spending time with me instead of his drinking mates. It was a pointless wish, and one I should've known not to harbour. That day ended as many others had before them, with me inside darning Jo's socks while the girls slept, and Jo out with his pals. Perhaps this next baby would bring us closer? I could only pray it would.

CHAPTER 15

Getting Married Again

August 1950 – Christmas Eve, 1953

There was the sound of a baby wailing. The high-pitched cry sounded through the thin walls. I opened my eyes, feeling Jo next to me deep in sleep. Without a murmur, I pulled off the blankets and walked, half-asleep still, into the adjoining bedroom. *How Jo can sleep through the baby's racket I'll never know*, I grumbled to myself.

It was early. The sky was still dark. I fumbled my way to the side of the cot where my new baby boy had been sleeping. Joseph, who was born on 16 May 1950 and was now three months old, was waving his fists, his eyes screwed up as he yelled for his next feed.

My girl Rita had run off to find the midwife when my contractions started, hurtling off with the pram for the gas and air machine! At the time I still couldn't believe we didn't have to find a shilling for the midwife to attend the birth. The National Health Service had been started two years previously and what a novelty, what a Godsend, that society's poorest, like us, didn't have to save up for a home birth, let alone a hospital delivery.

Times were changing. We could feel it even in the north of the country. Britain had felt like a battered, sagging beast for almost five years since the war ended. Our streets and the buildings in them were tatty, broken with war damage, their paint peeling, their exteriors unwashed and unloved. But we were resilient people, and what we lacked in money and things, we made up for in community and family life, however hard.

'There, there, don't cry little one, look, yer've gone and woken up the girls, like.' I whispered, hoping to mollify my son so that he'd fall back to sleep. Both Rita and Eileen were sat up in the bed they shared, rubbing their eyes.

'I need a glass of water,' said Rita, who was now twelve years old, as she pulled off her blanket and shuffled into the kitchen.

'Me too,' cried Eileen, her face puffy with sleep. Eileen was seven years old, and both girls had been delighted, and, I think, a little shocked, at the arrival of this boisterous boy with lung power to match. It had been a shock for all of us, but to be fair to Jo, he'd taken the news of my impending pregnancy in his stride, even boasting to his pals that he was 'growing a big family'.

'All right, our Eileen, Rita will bring you some water. Then back to sleep, eh? I'll take Joseph into bed with me,' and with that I carefully lifted him up, and carried him into Jo and my bed. It was a tight squeeze but I cradled my body round him and somehow we managed to get some more hours' rest, dozing until the early morning summer light crept into the room.

At 6 a.m. Jo woke up and got out of bed, dressing himself and reaching for his tobacco and heading to the lavvy. Leaving Joseph fast sleep, I wrapped my dressing gown round myself and went to the kitchen to put the porridge on for Jo's breakfast.

Jo usually left just before 7 a.m. He liked to have a shave every morning, and was always very particular about his clothing, even when he was in his workman's outfit of thick cotton trousers and a big overcoat. Without a word, my man sat down to eat, then when he'd finished he rolled himself a ciggie, lit it at the table and sucked in the day's first smoke. I rinsed his bowl, and poured him a cup of strong tea, just how he liked it. Then Joseph gave a howl, and at that moment, Jo got up, pulled on his coat and with a quick peck on the cheek, left for his day's work.

How I envied him his ability to sleep through the night without waking when our son yelled. He didn't seem to register it, and each morning he woke, refreshed, expecting his breakfast made and his tea poured, then he was off to work, without a care in the world! Life was very different for me.

My work never seemed to stop. If I wasn't feeding Joseph, I was washing out the clouts I used as nappies. I'd been down to the local market the week before his birth to buy an old sheet which I cut into squares, as I couldn't afford to buy the terry towelling ones I now saw in the shops. My handmade versions were barely adequate, and my days seemed to be filled with changing nappies, washing them and hanging them up to dry, which gave the house a permanent stale, dank odour that never seemed to disperse however much I aired the rooms.

I had the breakfast to make, porridge today with watered-down milk to make it go further. I hurried the girls off to school – though Rita wasn't far off leaving to make her way in the world – grabbed my basket and the pram, and grappled with my son to get everything down two flights of tenement stairs, before heading out to the local shops to see what I could pick up for dinner.

The square of tennies was busy with people going about their business. I said 'All right luv' to several of the other mothers as they too wrestled with little ones and prams. Now and then I waved as I saw women I recognised, standing round in clusters, all wearing the customary head scarves and hair rollers, catching up on the latest gossip, while trams thundered along the main road which was the Edge Lane tram route. Children were howling and screaming, already swarming over the play park on Hurst Gardens. I tutted, wondering why they weren't all at school, before crossing over the road to my stop.

Motor cars were now a familiar sight on the roads, moving at tremendous speeds, or so I thought! The tram pylons and wires criss-crossed over all our heads as we went about our business. Before long, we were rattling down the highway, heading down into the centre of Liverpool for me to change trams for Scottie Road.

Despite the chance to catch up with neighbours, and the brusque freshness of the day, my life sometimes felt relentless, especially with the lack of sleep following Joseph's birth, as I hadn't expected to be doing this again a third time. Life was tough, though I never complained, I didn't see the point. Everyone around here had the same worries. I didn't want to add to their burdens. I had plenty of opportunity to talk things through with my neighbours, as housewives popped in and out of mine and each other's flats most days, borrowing a cup of tea here or a slice of bread there. I didn't mind listening to others talk about their problems, but I generally took my own to my priest.

Today, I had decided to call in on Nellie and Da at Victoria Square, where they still lived. Nellie's eldest boy Tommy had fallen ill with tuberculosis and was convalescing at a hospital on the Wirral. Meanwhile, Nellie's husband Walter had jumped ship in New Zealand, going ashore on one of his sea missions and not coming back, despite the fact he had a wife and two boys: Tommy, five, and Walter eighteen months younger. Nellie's husband had been away so long that Tommy had thought that my da, Thomas Riley, was his dad! It broke my heart a little, knowing that. Walter Horrocks had been caught by the New Zealand authorities and been sent to jail for six months, and now he worked on a horse stud farm over there. Nellie had been surprisingly philosophical about her husband's abandonment of her and their children, insisting that if he came home she'd take him back without complaint.

I made the journey over to Da's as much as possible to see what help I could give, even if it was only moral support. I crossed the concrete area surrounded on all four sides with huge tenement blocks that stood four storeys high. It was another great effort to get Joseph, me and the pram up the steps to Da's flat, and by the time I got there I was breathless.

'It's me, our Maggie,' I called, carrying Joseph up the endless stairs.

Da was out at work, even though he was sixty-six years old. He never lost a day's graft in his life, if he could help it. Nellie was kneeling down, her scrubbing brush going great guns on the floor.

I tutted as I looked at the state of the place. Outside the tenements were black as the hobs of hell with soot and smoke. Rats sniffed through rubbish and water dripped down the walls. Despite the fact that Liverpool had appointed its first Medical Officer of Health in 1846, Dr William Duncan, and he had introduced sewers and drains to the city in a bid to eradicate cholera and diphtheria from the city stews, the buildings where people like us lived were still squalid, and diseases like TB were rife.

Nellie had given Da the bedroom, and slept with her son Walter behind the curtain in the main living room. The curtain blocked out the light, making the space feel even more constricted and forlorn, if that was possible. The walls were stained with brown, dirty water from the leaks in the roof, and bugs crawled everywhere, despite the hard work my sister did in trying to keep the place clean.

'All right, queen, how are ye?' I placed Joseph down on the freshly scrubbed floor, his big eyes taking in the room.

'Our Maggie, hello luv, I was just going to put the kettle on,' replied Nellie, getting to her feet and rubbing her back.

'Yer working too hard, queen,' I smiled. 'What's new then?'

'You won't believe this, but Walter says he's coming back from New Zealand. Got a letter from him the other day, like.'

I exhaled. Nellie was right, I didn't believe a word of it, but I didn't want to puncture her hopes either. 'That's news indeed, our Nellie. I'm made up for ye. I hope he means it, luv, I really do.'

I took off my coat and filled the kettle from the water jug. 'When are ye expectin' him, like?' I asked, trying to keep my voice light. I didn't want my sister to see my natural cynicism. Walter Horrocks had not exactly proved himself a good husband and father so far, but then, looking at my situation, I was hardly one to judge.

'Any day now. And Tommy will be coming out of the ozzy in the Wirral soon, so I'll have both my boys back at last.' Nellie's face was alight with hope, and as I looked at her I felt a sudden rush of protective love for her.

Nellie was a lovely young woman of twenty-two, with fairer hair than mine, and those beautiful blue eyes. She was devoted to her sons, and had visited Tommy without fail once a month, which was all she could afford. It had been a tremendous effort, saving her pennies, paying for the return fare for the ferry to Birkenhead then overland to West Kirby to the convalescing home for children. It must have broken her heart to be separated from her eldest boy, but she had young Walter and Da to care for, and could never have afforded to rent a room near to her poorly son, and so she selflessly accepted her lot, seeing Tommy whenever she could and never, ever complaining.

'And what's more exciting is that they're letting my

Tommy come home to me cos we're moving to a new council house in Speke! They said Tommy couldn't come back here due to the conditions and so they bumped us up the queue. It'll be a wrench leaving here, but I've seen a picture of the houses and they've got their own leccy and water, and there's even inside lavvies! Who'd have thought we'd ever have one of those!' With that, Nellie laughed delightedly.

'I'm made up for ye,' I repeated. What a turn up! An inside lavvy and electricity, it was tantamount to living in luxury. 'Ye'll be too good fer the likes of us, once you move to the posh house,' I joked, feeling happy that the boys and my sister would have a new home, and their family reunited.

It was very good news, though I couldn't imagine our father living anywhere except the area around Scottie Road. This part of north Liverpool, and the docks, were part of him, body and soul. They made him who he was. Without his Dockers' Union badge and his flat cap there was no Da. He was proud of his working life and he was a man born of the docks' shifting waters, as so many Scousers were. But, it was time we had sanitation. It was time our children breathed some fresh air and ran in the country around the new areas, so perhaps change was a good thing, for all of us, including our father.

Later that day, I returned home with a small lamb chop for Jo's dinner, and a couple of grey-looking sausages for the rest of us. That night, Jo came in as usual, took off his hat and coat, settled himself with a paper in front of the fire and lit a cigarette. I busied myself in the kitchen as I'd been out most of the day, rushing so Jo would have no complaints that his dinner was late. When we'd finished eating, Jo pushed his plate towards me as he usually did, but before I had the chance to take it, he grabbed my wrist and took hold of my hand.

I turned to him, unused to public displays of affection from Jo. It was different with our private life but we rarely showed any physical contact outside of the marriage bed. His face looked softer, his voice low and calm. I looked at him full in the face, searching for the meaning of this rare touch.

'I've been thinking, shall we get married?'

That stopped me in my tracks! I stood there, my face a picture of confusion, not quite believing the words that had just come out of his mouth. We'd been living together for eight years and had two children together. We'd never explicitly discussed getting wed, though I'd always assumed we'd get married one day in the future.

Time passed, everyday life had taken over, and so I'd put it to the back of my mind. Yet, it was something that niggled away at me. Without a wedding ring I had no security in our life together, no sense of permanence. Things weren't easy between us, I'd be lying if I said we were romantic together, but he was father to our children and getting married was the right and proper thing to do.

'Ye want us to get married, our Jo?' I asked at last, sitting myself back down. Some things were too important to hear standing up. I wanted to make sure I'd heard him correctly, it was so out of the blue, so unlike him to say it.

'Ye heard me, Maggie,' Joseph replied, sitting back in his chair and eyeing me with an amused expression. The Brylcreem in his hair looked shiny in the poor electric light.

'All right, our Jo, we'll get married, if that's what you want.' Was all I said. What else was there to say?

I felt happy that my children would be raised in a home where their parents were married. To say that I was thrilled to be marrying Jo, well I wasn't a lovesick young girl any more. I was a practical woman of thirty years old and the romantic part of me, if there ever was one, had been well and truly quelled by the years of childrearing, nappy washing and the sight of my man swaying like a reed in the marshes from his nights drinking down the pub. No, I wasn't one for fairy tales, but Jo was doing right by us all and so for that, at least, I was grateful.

I waited more than three years for Joseph's promise to become a reality. I'd like to blame our busy, hard-working lives, but at the end of the day, he didn't rush to make all the arrangements, and I decided not to push him in case he changed his mind. I wanted to be married as it represented security and living within our faith, but I wasn't a silly young girl with fancy notions of true love. I was a practical woman, and even though it frustrated me seeing Joseph stall for so long, I had to trust he'd do the right thing by us in the end. When he announced that we were to be married on Christmas Eve in 1953, at Brougham Terrace Registry Office in West Derby Road, I said a silent prayer to Our Lady in gratitude.

Da went ballistic when heard the news that we were getting wed in a registry office! It was the first time I'd ever seen him lose his temper so passionately. He swore using his own version of Jesus Christ.

'James's Church! They'd marry two donkeys in there!' he shouted, pulling off his cap and stamping it into the ground.

I tried to explain to Da that it was unlikely I'd be allowed to get married in a Catholic Church now, as a divorced woman, but for once he wouldn't listen. In fact, hearing about the registry office had brought up my own mixed feelings about getting married again, in light of my faith. Divorce was frowned upon, and it hurt me to think my next union would take place without the blessing of a priest, and the sacred rituals I held dear. Despite this, I did my best to look forward to our wedding day; after all, I would rather have a ring on my finger and my children secure than not.

The morning of the wedding eventually dawned, and after I'd sorted out everyone else, I finally had the chance to dress myself. Jo had bought me a new two-piece turquoise dress suit for the occasion and a hat with a blue feather on it. I was made up with that. It was the most luxurious outfit I'd ever worn, apart from my Holy Communion dress! I'd given birth to Dennis, or Denny as we affectionately called him, on 19 January 1953, and so had four young children, yet despite that I still had a lithe figure, kept trim by the hard work I did each day.

Gazing at the finished effect in the mirror, I saw a woman who was an echo of her former self. I looked at the small lines that had formed around my eyes. I smiled sadly at myself; I seemed a far cry from the young girl I still felt I was inside. Life had not been perfect. There had been no fairy tale ending. My charming handsome man was no prince after all, except to those he met outside our front door, behind it he was a different man, at times a cruel bully who taunted me and our children. Many would ask why I'd want to marry a man like that, but in those days our choices were limited. He provided for us and that had to be enough, I didn't expect to be happy with him.

There was no time to spend feeling sorry for myself on my second wedding day. I looked round at Rita, fifteen, Eileen, ten, three-year-old Joseph and eleven-month-old Denny, and felt proud of what I'd achieved. It may not have been riches but I'd got four beautiful children and each one of them was, to me, a gift from God.

My friend from the tennies, Annie Gorman, stood for me,

and by that I mean she acted as a witness, while one of Jo's work pals stood for him. We were a small party, just me, Jo, the babbies, Rita and Eileen, Da, Nellie and her boys. Nellie's husband Walter was also there. He'd finally returned home a couple of years earlier, and Nellie, being the sweet person she was, had welcomed him home without a murmur..

They'd moved to a new council home in Speke – a far cry from the flat in Hurst Gardens where Jo and I now lived – and Nellie was as happy as I'd ever seen her with her family together. And if Walter seemed stern and rather overbearing towards her, it wasn't up to me to point that out. Nellie was always a sunny, peace-loving character, and so I was happy for her that things had worked out the way they had.

After the ceremony, we didn't have the money to celebrate so we nipped into one of Jo's drinking haunts afterwards to have a drink and that was that, job done, after eleven years together.

When I watched Jo order another round for everyone with a great cheer from his pals, I felt familiar disappointment etch my soul. With a feeling of resignation, I turned and left.

I took the children home and settled them all in bed. I needed some time alone to go over the events of the day. For better or for worse, I was Jo's wife now, and I'd chosen my lot in life.

CHAPTER 16

Rent Day

July 1954

Bang! Bang! The sound of a fist slamming onto my front door in my Hurst Gardens flat almost made me drop the tea cups I was rinsing in shock. Another: *Bang!*

'Open up, Mrs Clarke, it's rent day and I haven't got all morning, like!'

I froze. Rent day! I'd clear forgotten. I knew without having to look that I didn't have the money. Jo had given me my housekeeping a week ago last Friday but hadn't left his usual family allowance, as he called it, last week and so I only had pennies left in my purse.

I looked around to see where the children were. They'd stopped playing and were staring at me, their eyes wide with fear. Even toddler Denny understood something 'bad' was happening as he was usually the first to make a racket. My four-month-old daughter Ann, baby number five, was asleep in the back bedroom and I was terrified the noise would wake her.

'Shhhhhhhh, keep still, don't say a word.' I put my finger to my mouth, making the age-old gesture for silence.

Eileen, eleven, wasn't at school today as it was wash day and I needed all the help I could get. It was normal at the time to keep daughters off school now and again. I didn't do it often, I wanted my Eileen to have a good education as she was a bright girl with a future ahead of her, but today I'd simply needed an extra pair of hands.

Bang! Bang! 'You in there, Mrs Clarke, yer rent's due. I'm a busy man so if yer in there please open up.'

The rent man, I never knew his name, was a shady looking character with deep set dark eyes and a way of holding his cap over his face so that he seemed permanently in shadow. He would be carrying a satchel stuffed to the gills with notes and coins, making his rounds. It wasn't the first time I'd pretended not to be at home when he called. Sometimes Jo spent all his wages and had nothing to give me, or sometimes he simply appeared to forget that I needed money for food and to keep this roof, however mean, over our heads. Cash was always tight for me, and today wasn't any different so there was nothing to do except hide and hope he went away quickly, though there was no chance of that. Those rent men could smell a fib from a mile off. They knew through experience who was bluffing and who might be hiding, it was like they sniffed the air for their prey. Or that's how it felt, as I cowered inside the scullery.

He banged again. He wasn't going to go away, so I motioned to Eileen to go and open the door. She looked at me, giving me one of her direct stares, then nodded. She knew without me having to tell her what she had to do. I watched my girl as she straightened herself up then marched over to the door, opening it with a flourish.

'What d'ye call this racket?' she countered.

I tried to sneak a look at the door but knew I didn't want to be caught hiding so I listened intently instead. There was a brief silence, she'd obviously caught the man off guard, and I almost chuckled. I had to whip my hand over my mouth to stop a giggle that bubbled up inside me. *Margaret Clarke*, I said to myself, sternly, *get over yerself, yer meant to be a respectable married woman, not a schoolgirl!*

I couldn't resist a quick glance round the doorway. Eileen

had one hand on her hip and the other holding tight to the door. She was clearly in control of the situation, and in that moment, even though we were telling necessary lies, I swelled with pride for her.

The man cleared his throat. 'All right, queen, I didn't mean to upset you, like, but it's rent day and yer rent is due so if you'd kindly fetch yer mam we can sort this all out.'

His voice was actually conciliatory! I could hardly believe my ears. The rent man was known for being pretty fierce and hard-nosed. His weekly visit was feared by the housewives as there were no excuses, no way of not paying. If you didn't have the money you were out on your ears, no matter what.

'Well, I'm sorry to disappoint ye but me mam isn't in, she must've forgotten, like. She's been busy with the babbies and sometimes it's all she can do to remember to put the dinner on the table,' Eileen said, this time more softly. She was buttering him up like a teacake!

'Oh well, I see. Well, sorry to disturb ye, didn't mean to alarm, but I'll need the rent so you'd better tell yer mam I called.'

The rent man's voice was gruff. He was apologising to Eileen; this was unheard of. *Even Jo'll get a laugh from this*, I thought.

Eileen tutted. 'Well, of course, I'll tell me mam. She'll be sorry to have missed you, like. She's got the rent money, don't fret about that, she's just out doin' the shopping so she must've forgot. Yer'll have to come back later.' Eileen's voice was firm, broking no argument.

I was just thinking we'd got clean away with it, when there was a sound from one of the bedrooms. It was Joseph. 'Mam, what you doin' there?' Joseph, or Joe as we now called him, who was four years old, had evidently had enough of the subterfuge and was in the process of blowing my cover.

He grinned as he scampered towards me, holding his arms out for a cuddle. I froze. My eyes wide as saucers, holding both my hands up to stop him and gesturing for him to go back to the bedroom, I stepped back, straight into my mop and bucket.

As if in slow motion, I watched as the long handle of the mop fell in a graceful arc. *Ah*, was all I could mouth as the impact of the handle against the stone sink sounded. *It's all over now, for sure*, I thought.

I didn't know what to do, and then Joe's voice could be heard again. 'Mam, play with me.'

Quick as a flash, Eileen ran over and scooped him up, clucking with him like a mother hen. 'You silly a'pporth, me mam's out getting the rations. What are you doing calling me "Mam", eh? Those pesky rats are knocking over the bucket again, I'll get me scrubbing brush out and chase them off!' She jiggled her brother in her arms as she spoke, distracting him, and hopefully the rent man as well! Joe collapsed into fits of laughter.

I could barely breathe. If the rent man knew I was hiding, not only would I look a fool and have to declare that I had no money, but it would all be round the neighbourhood by lunchtime. Clever Eileen for grasping the situation so quickly and pretending he was asking for her. The little ones did get confused, that was nothing new. Eileen was my helper and so she did lots of 'motherly' duties for the boys, such as shushing them to sleep, changing their clouts and walking them round the neighbourhood in the pram when they couldn't sleep. They often called her 'me mam Eileen' or 'me mam' by mistake. Even so, would the rent man fall for it?

Come on, our Eileen, shut that door and get that man away from this house . . . I thought to myself.

The seconds seemed to have stretched into minutes. At

201

least baby Ann had slept through the disturbance. At any moment Joe could blurt out my hiding place and our cover would be well and truly blown.

'OK, is that it? I'll be sure to tell our mam, thank ye, bye.' And with that, Eileen smiled politely then, with a firm hand, closed the door, immediately turning to me and hushing me. She even knew that my first instinct was to burst into cheers of relief, but it wasn't until she heard the shuffle of the man's footsteps move away from our door that we could all exhale.

My legs felt rather wobbly all of a sudden. I didn't know whether to burst into laughter or tears. I hated lying, I believed in speaking the truth, but we had to survive as well, and there was nothing I could do but enact this charade if I had no money to pay the man. He'd be back, I could be sure of that, but we had a few hours or days of grace, and in the meantime I had a worse job to do, I had to tackle Jo, my husband, head-on for the rent money, and I knew with a sinking feeling in my belly that it wasn't going to be easy.

'I need a cuppa, like, me head feels a bit woolly after that,' I exclaimed, feeling shaky, thanking God we had some sugar left as it would need to be a hot, sweet cup of tea to set me right again.

Our lives were continually shaped by our means. And when we had nothing, it became a battle for survival, a case of 'us against them', whoever 'them' may be. It was how I'd lived since a child, and I didn't expect it to be any different. Our small victories, such as today's, were set against a catalogue, a lifetime, of bigger losses. We knew we were powerless against the forces that shaped our existence; the government, the councils, the stevedores at the docks, rent men, and all the petty officials that we had to deal with. Without money we were like lambs to the slaughter, and it was only by the grace of God and the will to live each day that we got through. I had to draw on that strength for tonight's encounter with Jo. I knew that whatever I said I would be at fault. I knew that he would accuse me of spending the family allowance when I hadn't. I knew that it would take a superhuman effort on my part to stay calm and ask for what we needed.

Not for the first time in my thirty-four years, I wondered why life couldn't be a little easier. *Why, God, do I have these battles to fight, day in, day out?* I was tired, a little giddy after the earlier charade, and I just wanted to feel that I was making headway. With a sigh, I poured hot water into the teapot, watching the leaves swirl. I stirred the black tendrils, making a small whirlpool, and poured out the brown liquid. Circles of steam wound their way up to the ceiling.

I would have to think hard about what to say to my husband. But, for now, that and the washing could wait. And I had a souvenir copy of the *Picture Post*, dated 6 June 1953, to read. Borrowed from a kind neighbour, though it was a year old! I could finally catch up on the news that had gripped the nation at the time, Queen Elizabeth II's coronation on the second of that month. Over the months, the magazine had been passed carefully from hand to hand on the estate until everyone in the tenements had read it. I hadn't liked to put myself forward to borrow it, and it was only because my kind neighbour Annie pressed it on me, saying I was the last on the estate to read it, that I got the chance to catch up on the very old news.

I scanned the cover, a picture of the lion and unicorn emblem surrounded by a circle of colourful flowers. *What a treat!* Perhaps I would gain some sustenance from reading it, having a small bit of escapism, before tonight's inevitable showdown with my husband. But the sight of the coronation, and the happy faces in the crowds brought back memories of the actual day.

I remembered vividly the fact that ours was the only flat in the whole of Hurst Gardens that didn't have bunting or flags up outside (or inside) as Jo was fiercely anti-Royalist. Eileen had brought home a souvenir mug given to her at school. She was proud as punch of that mug, but as soon as Jo saw it he threw it into the bin, leaving our daughter in floods of tears.

I put the magazine down, suddenly unable to read it and shut my eyes. Leaning back on my chair I could hear all the usual sounds of the estate; children playing, house-wives shouting at their children, whistling as they hung out washing, the occasional radio turned up full volume by a near-deaf neighbour. Ordinary sounds of normal lives. It gave me strength to hear it. Whatever Jo thought about this or that, the world kept turning, children kept on playing and women kept gossiping and complaining about their 'arl fellas'. My home life was different in that it made me feel uncomfortable, and at times deeply unhappy, and yet I was still part of the life that hummed around me.

At that moment I heard a rap on the door, and Annie poked her head into my kitchen. 'Fancy a cuppa? See you at mine in ten minutes? Bring biscuits if yer've got them, queen . . .' Her voice trailed off down the landing the flats shared.

I sighed, stood myself up and brushed off imaginary dust from my apron, feeling a strange mixture of gratitude and sorrow. The chat would help, but I still had Jo to face tonight, and God only knew what kind of a fight that would be be-tween us. And it would be a fight, I was under no illusions. But it was a sunny day and I still had ten minutes to spare before popping over to Annie's, as Eileen was already chop-ping spuds for the scouse.

With a contended hum, I sipped my tea, stirring in plenty of sugar – thankfully no longer rationed – and opened the pages. The Queen's life was a million miles from my own, but leaving mine behind for a few moments wouldn't do me any harm. I hadn't heard the coronation on the wireless, we didn't have one, but I'd heard enough at the washhouse to know that the country had gone berserk for Elizabeth and her husband Prince Phillip. They seemed like a young couple in love, but more than that, they represented new times. A queen on our throne. We could hardly believe that a woman was at the helm of the nation, and a sensible, caring-looking woman as well. She couldn't do worse than some of our male sovereigns so her coronation was, to us, a symbol of rebirth after the grim war years. The ceremony had been lavish, a display of our country's fortitude and wealth, and perhaps, just perhaps, some of that good fortune and money would trickle down one day to the working man and his family. Anyway, it was a welcome break from the monotony of my daily routine, and I cherished it all the more knowing I had another cuppa with a friend to look forward to afterwards.

Later that day, after I'd given Jo his stew, cut and buttered his bread and sat watching as he finished everything on his plate, I plucked up the courage to tell him what had happened earlier. I picked at a thread hanging loose from my cardie as I did so, feeling nervous but determined to make Jo see sense about the money.

'Jo, the rent man came today,' I started, leaving a space for his reply. Instead, he grunted, as if to say, what's it got to do with me?

'Jo, I didn't have the money. We haven't paid our rent for this week and so I need it from ye tonight.' I could hardly believe my nerve, but better this than we lose the roof over our heads. Even so, my voice was more a whisper than a demand.

We had no security. We were entirely at the mercy of unscrupulous private landlords that stalked the poor in this city. Even now, in 1954, after much of the slum housing we all grew up in had been demolished and new housing built by the corpy, some of us still paid for private places as there weren't enough of the new ones to go round yet.

Jo pushed his plate towards me, leant back in his chair and gave me a long, hard look. With a strange half-smile, he looked away. Then, with a kind of slow satisfaction, he turned back, and this is what he said, 'What have you done with the money I gave you for housekeeping? Where's my money going, Maggie?'

He spoke slowly as if I was an imbecile. I bit my lip, trying not to look as desperate as I felt and drew in a breath to steady myself.

'Ye didn't give me no money on Friday. There was nothin' behind the clock when ye left fer the alehouse.' My voice was low, calm. I didn't want him sensing how frightened I felt because showing fear to him would only make it worse, he'd really go at me then like an animal hunting weaker prey.

'What am I hearing in my own home? Don't you tell me what to do, d'you hear me?' he hissed.

'I'm not telling ye what to do, Jo, I'm just sayin' that we haven't paid our rent fer this week and the rent man'll be back tomorrow so we'd better have it to pay him. I need that money, Jo.'

I crossed my arms in front of me as my body had started to shake. I hated these confrontations. They were a fact of our marriage, yet I could still never get used to them. Part of me thought that Jo thrived on the battles between us, or perhaps it was the drink taking its toll on his memory or state of mind. One thing was for sure, he was a perfect gent outside the home, so all of his meanness happened here, behind closed doors where no one apart from us could see it.

'If ye didn't spend yer evenin's down at the alehouses then we'd have the money to pay the rent. I'm sick of living like this, Jo, it's degradin',' I blurted out. I'd finally lost my cool, I could hold back no longer, especially seeing him dressed in his finery. It wasn't like me ever to lose my temper, but I'm not a saint and something inside me cracked a little that day.

Jo leapt to his feet. 'Holy Mary. Nobody tells Jo Clarke what to do, d'you hear me? Nobody. I didn't marry you to get nagged every time the kitty's short. You've spent my money and now you're asking for more.' This time he raised his voice, not loud enough for the neighbours to hear though, spraying spittle across the table.

He didn't usually shout, ever. He didn't need to. His sneers were usually enough to silence me, but not tonight, there was too much at stake.

With a small gesture, I wiped my face and stood up to face him, I didn't like sitting down with his tirade going on over my head. 'I didn't spend yer money Jo Clarke, and I want me housekeeping now for the rent and fer food, otherwise ye won't have any dinner tomorrow night. That's the last of the stew and bread. Give me my allowance Jo and ye can go off and do what you like with the remainder, but I won't let ye put our family at risk.' I stared him full in the face, unable to believe my determination.

He made a noise as close to a growl as I've heard a human make, and then, just as suddenly, he stomped over to his wool coat hanging by the door, pulled out his wallet and threw a handful of shillings onto the table. With a 'So help me God, I'm off to find better company than here ...' he stalked out of the flat, sweeping his smart new trilby onto his head and banging the door behind him. I felt like I'd been punched.

Just then, Eileen peered out from behind her bedroom door, her eyes widening as she saw the money lying on the table. She looked up at me and there was a smile on her face. 'Ye've won, Mam. Ye've got the rent money.'

I smiled weakly back at her. I'd got the money, and I'd made my point about the pubs and feeding our children, and what good it had done me? He was back out in the bars, probably buying drinks for his mates, all the while thinking he had been done wrong. I didn't know if the ale had really addled his memory, or whether the effect of it was to make him mean like that.

There were some nights, when he didn't drink, that he sat quietly by the fire darning his own socks without a murmur. He could be the life and soul of any party, and a generous man to his friends. Why then did we see this side to him? Why did he bring the bad moods home? Many nights I'd begged him to 'bring the good parts of you home, our Jo' and there were times when he was lucid that he agreed with me and said he was sorry and didn't know what came over him, but they were few and far between, and getting rarer by the year.

Our children were growing up and learning to flee from the sound of his boots on the threshold, to make themselves quiet somewhere so they didn't get a piece of his temper. I'd had to move Rita out of the house to a convent in Dover to keep her out of Jo's way, where she was now working in the kitchens for the nuns, such was his enmity towards her. That cost me my peace of mind, waving goodbye to my firstborn child. At the same time I was happy she was having her first taste of independence, and earning her own wage. How I'd longed to do that when I was Rita's age! This really was no way to live. Someone had to stand up to him, and that someone was me. It cost me dearly though.

I suddenly felt exhausted once all the fight had drained from me. I'd won a victory tonight, but who knew how many more skirmishes I'd have to fight over the years. I was wedded to him, for better or for worse, and nights like these it felt firmly like the latter.

CHAPTER 17

Call the Midwife

Christmas 1954 – 17 February 1955

Grabbing Ann, who was now almost a year old, wrapping her in extra blankets against the December chill, I picked up my purse and keys, swept a final look around my poky kitchen and, without acknowledging my husband, slammed the door behind me. As I started the descent down the two flights of stairs, which was especially awkward as I was seven months pregnant as well as carrying the baby, I could still hear Jo's raised voice, the scorn apparent for all to hear as he berated me for leaving.

This time I'd had enough. At long last, I'd woken up to myself and decided I couldn't stand another minute being belittled and criticised. It was Boxing Day 1954, and I'd just had the bleakest, loneliest Christmas of my life, despite the fact that I had been surrounded by my children and husband. It was a special time, the birth of Our Lord after Our Lady's labour trials. The story never failed to move me. A family unsettled, a woman about to give birth and nowhere to go, no home to feel safe in, and only God's love to guide them through those dark days.

As I reached the street, puffing with the exertion, I felt like I was in an exile of my own, a refugee from my difficult marriage to a man hell-bent on making me feel small and worthless. It was hard to describe how he did it. He rarely shouted, he didn't call me bad names or hit me. But with the curl of his lips or the cold stare of his eyes, he made me shrink further into myself with each passing day. I can only describe it by saying that he undermined me, telling the children to do the opposite of what I'd said, telling me I was no good as a wife or mother. Nothing you'd go to the law and complain about, but enough damage over time to shred my dignity, my sense of self, to the point that I was desperate enough to leave.

And there was the fact of the money. He never gave me enough, only half of his wages, if that, every week. To buy clothes for the children I was having to pay a little every week to the Provy lady, the nickname we gave to the woman from doorstep lender Provident Financial who lent small sums at high interest rates to the poorest of society, while Jo was the best dressed man in Old Swan. It didn't seem right, and I was sick of asking for more money and being told I was wasteful with the little he gave me. He was tight. I'd even go as far as to say that he was selfish, though I appreciated that he gave me something.

I was going to my sister Nellie's place in Speke, and hailed the number 500 bus as it rumbled to the stop. I wiped a quiet tear from my eye as I sat, holding my huge belly and shushing Ann as she took to wailing for her next feed. It was moments like these that Our Lady's tribulations felt close, familiar even. I couldn't have imagined how she must have felt to give birth in a stable, far from home, with a husband who had doubted her but was sticking by her nonetheless. It was a part of the great mystery that was God's plan, and I couldn't help but muse on it as the bus gathered speed through the empty morning streets. A woman in my position should've been at home now, cooking late breakfast for her children and husband, enjoying the time together as a sacred bond of family and community. But here I was, crying on a bus taking me out of the city to the only other family I had.

*

It had all started on Christmas Eve, which began nicely enough with Jo coming in early at six o'clock after a few scoops in the nearby pub. I was pleased he'd decided to come home for us all to spend the evening together.

'Here you are, a Christmas present for my wife,' laughed Jo, handing me a wrapped gift. It felt light and rather squishy, and I smiled in happiness, thinking perhaps things were starting to change for us. Jo was at the 'life-and-soul' stage of the drinking, full of good cheer and making the children giggle with tales of his exploits in Ireland.

I looked on my family fondly, hoping against hope this meant that the Jo I met, the charming, caring man who courted me so swiftly, was back at last. 'Go on, girl, open it will you!' Jo beamed, giving me his customary wink. His face was lined and flushed red with the ale but he was still a handsome man, always the most imposing wherever he was with his height and ebullient character.

'But it's not Christmas yet, like,' I giggled, feeling like a naughty young girl for unwrapping my present before Christmas morning. In my hands sat a pair of snug slippers, just the right size.

'Put them on, and show me,' he commanded, so I obliged, standing up and wiggling my toes.

'They're nice, thanks luv, a good fit,' I replied, blushing a little with the attention.

'Now then, I'm off for a few scoops, I promised the boys but I wanted to give you those before I left.'

I should've known, but this latest blow left me reeling.

'But it's Christmas Eve, Jo,' was all I managed to say, and there must've been something in my voice, the tone of it, something that changed him from the happy husband he was playing, back to the tyrant I lived with.

He turned, and his stare was as icy as the air outside our window. 'You don't tell me what to do, wife. All I want is to have a few scoops with the lads but you don't like it, you never like it when I try and enjoy myself do you, Maggie.' It wasn't a question. It was a statement, and he was right.

'I don't like it tonight, Jo.' My voice was small. I hated hearing the fear in it.

He pounced on it, stepping closer, and in a low voice, he whispered that I didn't deserve my slippers, I didn't deserve any presents, because I was a bad wife, and my whole purpose was to ruin his enjoyment of the Christmas spirit. I wanted to run then, but I felt rooted to the spot. Unable to move away from the poison he was pouring in my ears. At least none of the children could hear. They were all oblivious, bored of the slippers and back to playing amongst themselves in their bedroom. Only I heard his words, only I felt the long, slow deflation of a balloon as it loses its shape. I sank into myself and sat down. This seemed to spur him on.

Fuelled by his own self-righteous anger, he suddenly grabbed the slippers and pulled them off my feet.

'What are ye doin' Jo?' I gasped.

'Watch me,' was all he said as he dropped the slippers with casual cruelty onto the fire. 'No, Jo, me slippers, like.' I let out a noise that sounded like a sob.

Powerless, I stood and watched as my Christmas present caught the flame, flaring brightly in the grate. 'Me slippers,' I moaned. My present. Gone.

I turned back to Jo. He was watching my face as it crumpled. With a satisfied grunt he settled back down onto his chair and opened the day's *Liverpool Echo* as if a pair of footwear burning on the fire was a completely normal event. He even changed his mind about going out, preferring to stay in our small lounge with the slippers burning in the fire, almost like he was savouring the moment.

After that, I went through Christmas as if underwater. I tossed and turned all night, sleeping little, while having to lie next to Jo who was snoring peacefully. Christmas morning, Jo woke and acted as if nothing had happened. He was cheerful and gregarious, enjoying his Christmas morning, chasing Joe and Denny, who were four and almost two, and singing carols at the top of his voice.

As the winter sun rose, I got up, rubbing my back, sore from my sleepless night, and aching from the weight of the baby, and went into the living room. My slippers were still smouldering in the grate, the smell of them burning turned my stomach and I could've wept like a child. Of course, the children knew nothing of this and I had to spend the day acting as if everything was normal, but inside something cracked. This latest piece of theatre was too much for me. I'd longed for a comfy pair of slippers to keep my feet warm, and more than that, I'd longed for a kind word or gesture from my husband. Something in this event had shown me, as if for the first time, that I wouldn't get that, perhaps I'd never get that again from him, and so I decided to go. It wasn't a rational decision. I'd have to leave behind my children, Eileen, eleven, Joe and Denny, for the while but I couldn't stay there a moment longer.

So, on Boxing Day morning, I calmly got up out of bed, packed a small suitcase, dressed Ann and wrapped her up, then said to Jo that I was leaving. At first he laughed. Then when he saw the look on my face, my sheer determination, he started to get upset, telling me I was bad mother to my children, a bad wife to him. The usual insults, but this time the words rolled off me like raindrops. I turned my back to him and walked out, hoping against hope that he wouldn't try to follow me. He didn't.

Later that day, when I knocked on Nellie's door, we stared at each other for a moment. Without a word, and with full understanding, she gestured for me to go inside. Nellie's boys Tommy, nine, and Walter, eight, were playing in the living room with a mechanical lorry that must have been their Christmas present.

'Make yerself comfortable, queen. Do ye want a cuppa?'

I shook my head.

'I was just singin' the boys a song, does baby Ann want to hear it?' Nellie said kindly.

She was known for her small height, at five foot two inches, and for her beautiful singing voice. Nellie had inherited that from our mam, one of the few good things she left us, in my view. I nodded, unable to speak. If I'd opened my mouth a crack, I swear I'd have burst into unhappy tears and I didn't want to do that to Nellie and her family at Christmas. She sang:

What will I do when I get home and what will me
    father say,
He bought a jug from China, many a thousand miles
    away,
I met some naughty boys in the road and they kissed me
    as a joke,
So I boxed their ears for spillin' the beer, and that's how
    the jug got broke.

She finished and I laughed. Her voice had the soft lilt of the Irish, picked up from Mary Mullen, our mam who was of Irish descent, as she sang an old song from Scotland Road that referred to the jugs of ale that children were often sent to the pubs to fill up before their father got home. It was a throwback to earlier times, when children walked barefoot through the cobbled streets in rags, their hair matted, their faces grubby. Days when men who couldn't find work slumped on street corners, smoking ends of cigarettes, while housewives in long black skirts and shawls chatted as they carried their bundles of washing or shopping, their urchin children playing hopscotch in the passageways that wove in and out of the filthy, overcrowded courts at the turn of the century.

We lived like that too, and though it was a disease-ridden mess of people, dirt and vermin, they'd been our streets, our courts, our whole world, and it was a strange comfort to hear that familiar song now.

'Mam used to sing that song to us as babbies, d'ye remember,' smiled Nellie.

'I do, she'd sing it when we couldn't sleep,' I replied. 'We still didn't sleep but it was nice, like.'

Nellie spoke in a soft voice. She told me then that she'd been to see Mary, taken Tommy and Walter with her. I didn't know it, but apparently Mary had only moved a few streets away from Athol Street when she left us for her fancy man. They'd had three children together, all girls. For a moment, neither of us spoke. How had I not known that she was living so close to us? Perhaps, our narrow courts and towering tenements were capable of keeping their secrets after all? Perhaps Mary hadn't wanted to be found, perhaps she gave out to her neighbours that it would upset her first family if we knew she hadn't gone far?

I didn't know the answers, and I wasn't sure I wanted to know, either. All my feelings about my mam's abandonment of us had been locked away for many years now and I didn't want to reopen them. If Nellie wanted to see her then that was up to her, but I knew that it wasn't for me and mine.

Just then, little Ann stirred. She'd fallen asleep on the bus, and her gentle snufflings soon became insistent cries for her next feed. It was enough to distract us from talking about our uncomfortable past.

'Better get the dinner on or the boys'll be hungry.' Nellie got up and headed to the kitchen, leaving me to ponder how bizarre life could be.

Two days later there was a knock at Nellie's door and I went over to open it. Eileen stood there brandishing a handwritten note. I could see without having to open it that it was Jo's scrawl.

'Mam,' was all she said. I let her in and gave her a kiss. 'I've missed ye Mam, when are ye comin' home?'

That was hard to hear, but I hadn't softened to Jo yet. Reluctantly, I opened the missive. It read like a romantic novel, promising me that things would be different from now on if only I'd come home. I sighed. If I was honest, I knew I'd have to go back eventually. I couldn't abandon my children, however unhappy my marriage was. It wasn't natural. I couldn't do to them what my mam did to me, Nellie and Tommy, could I? When I read the note, and heard the plea in Eileen's voice, I knew my time away from home was over, for now. I had to go back, whatever it cost me. History couldn't, and wouldn't, be repeated. I, of all people, knew the damage that a mother leaving her children could wreak on their hearts.

That was not the last time I left, though. Several times over the years, I found the courage to flee to Nellie's and, each time, Jo promised me the earth to win me back. I would go back and, for a few days, Jo would avoid the alehouses and stay at home, acting in a conciliatory and polite way towards me. But the urge for the drink would pull him back into those bars, and before I knew it the Jo I learned to hate returned, stinking of booze and full of disdain.

It was February 1955, the wind was bitter and each morning I shivered as I bent down to light the fire in the grate. The baby would be here soon enough, but I had a few days to get things done, so I hastily spring-cleaned the flat and scrubbed down the floors in preparation.

I was sure I wasn't due for at least a week, but one evening, on 16 February, I started feeling that strangeness that comes on just before a baby arrives. It is a feeling like wanting to hibernate, crawl into a dark, warm space and birth my baby privately.

Overnight the pains came on but I managed to doze fitfully through them, thinking that the fake contractions had gone on longer, and were stronger, than they'd ever been before. It wasn't until the grey light had finally reached the skies the next morning, that I realised these weren't fake contractions, they were the real thing. Even so, I didn't want to panic my husband so I carried on with my day, knowing that these things took time, and, again, not unduly panicked.

By the time Jo returned from work, via the alehouse, of course, things were well on their way. The contractions were coming every few minutes. Despite that, I still didn't feel rushed. I'd birthed five babies so I knew a thing or do about it!

'Jo, go and call the midwife!' I panted as he walked in.

He blinked, took in the sight of me crouched over the iron bedframe, and exclaimed, 'Holy Mother of Christ!'

At that moment I let out a long moan. Without another word, Jo raced from the flat, staggering slightly I noticed. He looked worse for wear with drink but I had no time to worry about that.

I had started getting the urge to push so I knew things had speeded up faster than I'd anticipated. I leant over and started to groan as my body gave way to the rising urges. The contractions engulfed me, driving my mind inwards, into a place of pure sensation. 'Call the midwife now!' I wailed. This baby was coming fast, there was no stopping it.

Jo was back a few minutes later, clearly out of breath. 'Maggie she's coming, the midwife's coming, now that's it girl, take it easy for a second.'

I looked up at Jo gratefully, I didn't want to be on my own while I waited. It wasn't usual for a man to be at his child's birth in those days, but as the next contraction hit I held onto his hand squeezing it for all it was worth. I heard him inhale as I crunched his hand but I couldn't stop, my body had taken charge and was forcing this child out into the world.

Just then there was a knock at the door and a neighbour poked her head round the door, 'Midwife's arrived, she's almost at the tennie door.'

Joseph ran down the stairs. I waited, hoping and praying she would be quick getting up here. But no one arrived. I gave another push, falling to my knees, and surrendering to my body as it did sacred work, expelling our baby.

Just then Jo appeared at the doorway, slurring as he boasted that he'd chased away the midwife on her bike! At first I thought he was joking, then, as I waited for the uniformed nurse to appear, the seconds and minutes ticked past and I realised he'd actually done what he'd said he had.

'Jo, what did you say to my midwife? Why's she not comin'?' I said between contractions, holding my hip and I breathed.

'Don't go nagging me, Maggie, I didn't like her so I told

her to get going,' he replied, not meeting my fierce gaze.

'What do you mean, you didn't like her? What happened Jo?' I said, not caring if it upset Jo. He was easily upset, his sensibilities, though insensitive to everyone around him, were heightened and tender towards himself.

'She didn't show me no respect,' slurred Jo, his eyes blood-shot from the ale.

'For heaven's sake Jo, I'm havin' a babby. Couldn't you have forgiven her this once, and thought of me instead of yourself for once?!' I exclaimed, angry now and more than a little tired of Jo's defensiveness.

Before Jo could snap back at me, I doubled over again, a long 'ooooooooooh' coming from my mouth.

'It's comin' Jo, it's comin, yer goin' to have to help me if there's no midwife.'

My husband's face bleached white. He looked momentarily confounded. Then, to his credit, he knelt down next to me and started stroking my back.

'The baby's comin' now, Jo, I need you to help me.' I was fierce with the force of the pressure on my body. We needed to get to work as I couldn't hold on any longer.

In a few moments it was all finished. Jo was crouched on all fours, holding our newest little one, a girl who was screaming at the top of her tiny lungs.

'Is she OK?' I said, my legs trembling beneath me, and feeling for the baby's head.

'She's a beauty, so she is,' was all Jo said. I looked round. He was cradling our daughter, his face alight with happiness and something else, a kind of shock. He'd done it, he'd delivered our baby, goodness knows how, but she was safe.

Just then there was a knock at our front door, and a different midwife, an older lady, appeared in the bedroom doorway. 'Goodness!' she said.

She was a rather plump woman with an air of competent bustle about her. 'Thank you, Mr Clarke, I'll take it from here,' she said, carefully taking hold of the baby.

Jo was as meek and mild as a tiny kitten. Without a murmur about 'respect' he edged out of the room, looking almost shamefaced as he did so. I didn't have the energy to worry about his reactions, though.

As Jo left, she turned to me. 'Well done, Mrs Clarke, you've been very brave, very brave indeed. Now let's finish up and get you both cleaned and settled.'

I closed my eyes. It was good to be looked after, even for a few brief moments. As she placed my newest daughter into my arms, I felt that swell of joy that only a new baby can bring.

'You look like a Kathleen,' I murmured, stroking her little face, 'and yer a lucky girl being brought into the world by yer daddy.'

Jo, for all his faults, had stayed with me and had seen it through to the end. Today, he'd done his daughter proud. And we had that rarest of moments, a sense of wonder that we experienced together as he held our girl and felt the awe of a new life entering the world. We'd smiled across at each other, then looked into little Kathleen's screwed-up face.

'She looks like her mammy,' Jo had said, and even though it didn't erase the troubles and emotional hurts he'd inflicted on me for years, it went some way to healing my heart that day.

CHAPTER 18

Moving Day

November 1956 – 1960s

Not surprisingly, the peace between Jo and myself didn't last long. He soon went back to his old ways, which by now I'd learned to tolerate. Then in 1956, Jo put our names down for a new council house in Kirkby, where the council had built overspill estates to house those affected by the Blitz. We were delighted when our application was successful. I could hardly believe our luck; the new houses had running water, electricity and indoor bathrooms! No longer would I have to lug prams, bags and children up and down tenement steps, no longer would we be prey to unscrupulous landlords and rent men who banged on doors and frightened me out of my wits. We would be tenants of the corpy, and at last it felt like something had gone right for us as a family.

That feeling didn't last long. As the moving date drew near, I packed what I could into boxes, with breakables wrapped in old newspaper, but I had children to look after so I had to rely on Jo to sort the furniture and bigger items. My husband had booked a removal man with an open wagon to come early on the day of our departure.

Waking up on the day we were due to relocate, I was surprised to find the space beside me empty. Jo was nowhere to be seen. *That's odd*, I thought, it wasn't like Jo to be up early before me. He usually lay there dozing until I'd made breakfast and lit the fires, especially as the mornings were cold now. 'He must be packing up downstairs,' I muttered to myself, distracted immediately by eight-month-old baby

Kevin who had followed Kathleen by just over a year, arriving on 8 March 1956, and was now getting ready for his next feed by making whimpering noises. I hushed him, picked him up and carried him to the kitchen, yawning. Kevin was my seventh baby. It was hard to believe I had carried and birthed six others! They certainly kept me busy.

It was an exciting day, though. I stumbled across the kettle, lit the cooker and waited for it to boil, then padded into the children's bedroom to see them all lying higgledy-piggledy together in the one bed, arms flung over each other's bodies, their pink faces angelic in the morning light. I stood there for a moment, watching them, delighting in their innocence, their ability to live in each moment as if it was their last. The real world would be waiting for them outside of these walls but not yet, not yet. I wanted to stop the world turning, let them sleep for a while, but there was too much to be done and we had to crack on.

'Come on, up ye get you lot, it's movin' day,' I said in a sing-song voice.

From the kitchen the kettle started its high-pitched note and I hurried back. It was at that moment I realised I hadn't seen Jo in the flat. Where could he be? *Must be using the lavvy along the communal hallway*, I thought, then busied myself getting the breakfast porridge on the table, one ear alert for sounds of his footsteps at the doorway.

Half an hour passed, and there was still no sign of him. *The removal man'll be here any minute*, I worried. I wasn't sure what to do if my husband wasn't here. Do I move or should we stay there and wait? Had something happened to him? I felt the first icy pangs of fear in my stomach but there was too much to do to give in to them. I decided it was best to get us all ready and get on with things. Perhaps Jo had left already for the new place, and was waiting for us there?

'Well, he could've told me, like,' I muttered to myself irritably. I had my hands full, and Jo not being here meant extra work for me. Goodness knows how that poor removal man would get everything out of the place without another man to help.

The day felt like it was going sour and it was only eight o'clock.

'Get dressed, all of ye, the older ones help the little 'uns,' I clapped my hands, we had to get ready quickly. I didn't want the man turning up and finding me with my nightie on! Quick as a flash I got changed, made sure all the children had decent dresses or trousers and cardigans on and their shoes. It was a chill November day.

The bang at the door announced Bill, the man who Jo had hired to help. I answered it, and he looked around, puzzled. 'Yer not ready, like. Where's yer husband, and why's the furniture not piled up to move, eh?' he was abrupt, but I couldn't blame him.

'The furniture?' I answered, shaking my head. 'What should we have done?'

'Yer husband said it was a quick job, he'd pile up the furniture and we'd move it downstairs together, but he's not here and nothin's ready!'

I looked at the dishevelled room, then back at the man. He was of short stature, with a broad back and a woodbine hanging from the corner of his mouth. He wore a cloth cap and a thick coat. I must've have looked as crestfallen as I felt, as he added, more kindly,

'Come on then, Mrs Clarke, Jo or no Jo, we best get this stuff out.'

I looked at him gratefully, then gathered the children together and gave them the smaller things to carry.

'Be careful,' I called as they made their way down the

stairs, chattering. Up in the flat Bill was already heaving one of the mattresses out. It took several hours, and many swear words uttered by Bill, to get all of our furniture onto the wagon. Two bed frames, two mattresses, the kitchen table, chairs and various bits and bobs perched awkwardly on the back. The man was sweating heavily, and so I made him a cup of tea that he finished in one gulp, before we all hopped on board and drove off to Kirkby.

Jo must be waitin' at the new place, I said to myself, *where else could he be?* Despite my attempt at bravery, deep down my heart had sunk to my stomach. Jo had made many promises he hadn't kept over the years, but not to turn up on our moving day, when I could hardly be expected to lug bed frames, well, that was something else.

We arrived and Bill left the wagon in front of the house that was to be our new home, one of a group of similar-looking houses on our new estate. Everything was brand new, from the taps to the light switches, and the children ran through it exclaiming with delight. Even the paint was wet on the front door! I stepped inside, everything seemed to gleam at me, and for a second I forgot all about Jo's disappearance and sank into the moment. Winter sun streamed in through the new glass window, and looking round I couldn't believe my eyes when I saw we had four bedrooms. Four bedrooms! I felt like a real queen! Denny had fun flushing the new toilet, until I shouted at him to stop. Joe was screaming with pleasure as he spotted the small garden out the back. Life seemed to finally have dealt us a winning card, and yet my husband still wasn't there.

Luckily he'd given me the key and the address the night before, just before he headed out to the pubs. I hadn't thought anything of it. He went out most nights now and relations between us, despite the babies that arrived every year (or so it felt!), were at an all-time low. He could hardly speak to me without complaining, and I shrank more and more into myself, avoiding contact with him whenever I could, and feeling more and more like he was married to the ale rather than me.

I looked round to see Bill dragging things off the wagon, but instead of carrying them into the house, he left them on the patch of grass outside our front door. The bed frames and mattresses were pulled off and dumped out the front along with the table and chairs and all our boxes. When at last he finished, he turned round and got into the vehicle, starting the ignition and pulling on his cap.

'But aren't ye carryin' everything inside?' I asked, running up to his cabin.

He wound down the window and shook his head. 'If yer husband can't be bothered to be here to move his things then I'm not doin' it. I'm not bein' paid enough to haul them in again by meself. Sorry, Mrs Clarke, but this is as much as I'm doin' today.' He wound the window back up, tipped his cap to me, his eyes not meeting mine, then he drove off, leaving me standing by a great pile of our things wondering how on earth I was going to get them inside.

Fighting back angry tears, I called to Rita and Eileen, and together we dragged one of the mattresses into the lounge. We huffed and puffed, and hauled the thing through the small front door and let it flop onto the new linoleum flooring. We each collapsed on top of it, giggling as we lay there, looking up at our new lounge ceiling.

Despite the moment of jollity, it was a strange day that left me feeling like a widow rather than a wife. Jo eventually appeared later that night, with no apology or explanation except the smell of stale beer and tobacco on his breath. Our first night as a family in our new home was another exercise in keeping the children jolly while making excuses for their father and his drinking. I scraped together a basic dinner of beef dripping butties and settled the children down on that mattress, piling blankets on top of them to keep out the cold. I carried some of the boxes in but left most of our things outside. I didn't have the energy or the strength to carry in furniture, and so, despite the impression it must've given our new neighbours, I allowed myself to worry about them later.

Everythin' will be better tomorrow, I told myself, but in my heart of hearts, I didn't really believe it.

The next day, Jo acted as if nothing had happened, but I expected that by now, born of bitter experience. I still felt unable to speak to him. I was so upset about his casual abandonment of us on such a special day. He whistled as he shaved, wolfed down his porridge and left for work. I watched him go. Jo had upset the children and me many times in the past, and perhaps I was too sensitive to him and his ways, and perhaps I did nag him a bit now and again, but this time, something felt different.

My feelings for him changed that day, I can't say why or how, but they crystallised into something verging on hatred. He was still a good-looking man, bright and full of the gregarious charm of the drinker, and I'd always remember the man I met back in wartime, that echo of the love I'd felt for him when he swept me off my feet. But now, I could finally acknowledge to myself that I'd lost that feeling for good. Any love, any residual warm feelings for him, any sense of a wifely duty, had gone forever. Perhaps I realised for the first time that I could manage perfectly well without him? Perhaps it was just one more hurt piled on top of many, many others over our long relationship? Who can say? As I stood at the sink and watched the departing frame of my husband from my lovely new kitchen, on a day that should've been a joyous one, I vowed that I would never let him make me unhappy again. I found the first seeds of the strength inside me that would carry me into my own future, but that was still to come.

The years passed and little changed. My children were no strangers to the influence of The Beatles, the boys from Liverpool who in the early 1960s were taking the world by storm. My boys loved the movie *A Hard Day's Night*. With it came a sense that young people could be who they wanted to be, could stand up in the world and be themselves in ways unimaginable to my generation. I saw the new confidence exposure to these four lads who grew up in our city gave my children.

As my boys grew older, they saw how Jo treated me and they became protective, and that caused a lot of fights with their father. I trembled for them, though. I knew how spiteful my husband could be, and I knew how fragile this young energy was, but also that I couldn't interfere for fear of damaging my boys' self-esteem forever.

One Christmas, our Joe bought his first girlfriend Val over for us to meet her. His father Jo had been out drinking, and on his return he staggered in laughing and carousing, then stopped the minute he laid eyes on the poor young girl. My son Joe must have been fifteen years old or so, his girlfriend the same age, and for some reason my husband took an instant dislike to her.

'Who is this in my home at Christmas?' Jo slurred, his face contorted by drink.

'Me girlfriend, Father. Her name's Val and she's here for dinner, like.' Joe stood tall as he faced up to his father's odd and distinctly hostile behaviour.

'Well she's not welcome! Who d'you think you are coming

here uninvited?' Jo rounded on her, pushing his face into hers.

The girl backed off, gripping Joe's hand, but my son, despite his tender years, stood his ground, bless him.

'Yer insulting the girl I luv,' he said, with fierce pride.

I loved him like a tigress in that moment. My boys were growing up, and this was the proof.

Then, without warning, Joe hit his father full in the face. We all gasped. The boys had been standing up to their father more often, but this was the first time violence had broken out. It wasn't pleasant and I'm not saying that Jo didn't deserve a dressing down, by God he did, but I'd have done anything to stop my sons having to do this to the man who was supposed to love them.

Of course, my son left, taking his shocked girl with him, and Jo, looking more puzzled by now than angry, slumped into the sofa without a word. We all tiptoed round him even more than usual that Christmas, not wanting a repeat performance.

But deep down inside me I was glad my husband had got his comeuppance at last.

CHAPTER 19

Epiphany

1963 – 1970s

I held Da's roughened hand, waiting for another coughing bout to subside, his face wrinkled and lined, screwed up in pain.

'Da, let me help you,' I implored, leaning forward to try and help him, but he waved me away with his free hand.

'Da, ye always were the most stubborn man I ever met,' I whispered, as tears streamed down my face. I turned away, not wanting him to see my distress, but I was too late. He squeezed my fingers, his digits gnarled and craggy. It was his way of trying to reassure me, and fervently I wished he could.

He lay with his head against the clean fluffed-up pillows of the hospital bed, his eyes sunk into his face. I stroked his hand tenderly, hoping he could feel the love I had for him.

When he cleared his throat, I offered him the glass of water that sat on his bedside table, but he shook his head. Fighting for breath he tried to sit up, I reached over to stop him but he waved me away again.

'Maggie, luv, I want to say something, it might be the last chance I get,' he whispered.

I shook my head, 'Don't say that, Da,' and I could hear my voice crack with emotion.

'Our Maggie, I know I've stood silent for years about Joseph, but if I don't speak now I'll go to my grave regrettin' it.'

I had a feeling I knew what he was going to say.

'Me lovely girl, ye were always the prettiest, the most loving girl a man could have as a daughter. But why ye threw yerself away on that man, I'll never know.' His voice grew stronger as he spoke the words that were so difficult to hear. 'He was never good enough for yer, Maggie, and he don't treat yer right. You know it yerself. Now, I want you to do somethin' for me, will you promise?'

'Anythin', Da, anything for ye,' I replied, dreading the words he was about to say.

'I want ye to stand up for yerself, Maggie, and if he don't like it then ye have me blessing to leave him.'

At that I gasped. Da was firmly religious. Divorce to him was an anathema. I could hardly believe he'd given me permission to leave my second marriage.

'Don't worry yerself, Da, I'll be OK,' I answered feebly.

Even though he was deaf, he could lip read, and he could see by my face what I was saying. 'Ye know what I'm sayin'?' he asked.

I nodded my reply, tears streaming down my cheeks.

Da shut his eyes, knowing that he'd said what he had to say but it had cost him his last ounces of strength.

We'd both known he was dying. The doctors had said there was nothing more they could do for him. He was suffering from a weak chest, brought on from years of backbreaking labour and cancer of the liver. Over the days and weeks he had lain in his hospital bed, I'd watched my seventy-nine-year-old Da contracting, shrinking, into an old, decrepit man.

I clasped his hand as it lay on the crisp, white sheets, hoping against hope we were all wrong and he'd outlive us all, as I'd always joked he would. But it was clear that he had only hours left to live. I hushed him when he tried to speak again, telling him to save his energy.

'We all love ye, Da, more than ye can imagine,' I said,

gazing into his face, his eyes closing, his breathing becoming a rasping shadow of life.

'Go to God, Da. He's waitin' fer ye, ye've made him wait a long time, an' now yer work here is done. There'll never be a man more loved born on this earth, Da. Go now, go to God, with our love.'

My words seemed to settle him. His breathing lengthened but his eyes shut for the last time. As the sun set on that day in 1963, Da's life gently left him, his spirit returning to its holy source, the God we believed in so strongly. In the moment he left, I felt something shift, a freeing of his spirit perhaps, or a sly breeze maybe. Whatever it was, I knew he'd gone before the nurses had checked, before I felt for his missing heartbeat.

Only my faith saw me through those next days and weeks, and the love and support of Nellie, and our children, his grandchildren. We told them all how loved they had been by their grandda, and we all wept together, remembering a man devoted to his family, and to his faith.

Though I grieved terribly for him, I also wanted him to be free of this world that had treated him with such callous disdain. Throughout his gruelling work, his dreadful injuries, the poverty that he never escaped from, the death of his only son, and the desertion by the woman he adored, he never complained. He never bemoaned his lot. He accepted his fate with the resilience, fortitude and dignity of the proper working classes, those of us who grafted and lived with pride because of it, those of us who could barely afford a heel of bread and the shoes on our feet, those of us who knew what it was to be cold and hungry, yet we yearned to live each day.

A few weeks later, Nellie and I went through his things, little though there was left by him. In the hallway, in all the places we'd lived as a family, there had been a small mirror hanging up, engrained with grime and etched with time so that it was barely able to show us our reflection. On taking it off the wall of Nellie's home in Speke, we discovered that attached to the underside of the mirror Da had kept his wedding photo, from that fateful day in 1916 when he and Mary were two hopeful young people filled with love. Da had never discarded the picture, even when Mary left him.

Seeing that black-and-white photograph, and knowing how much family meant to my father, was the moment I let my grief flood from me in a spasm of tears. Nellie and I were the custodians now of our father's few things – his snakeskin wallet, his remaining coins, his photograph, flat cap and braces, along with the medals our brother Tommy won during the Second World War – and together we said goodbye at last to our beloved, kindly dad. If only Jo had been more like him, my life could have been so very different.

'D'ye remember, queen, when Da used to tell me off fer me cookin'?' laughed Nellie at last, choking a little from her crying. 'He'd wipe his mouth, say, "That was very nice our Nellie but don't make it again."'

'Oh yes, he was a one, wasn't he! He'd think you'd been extravagant with the housekeeping if it tasted good,' I replied. 'Didn't like spendin' a ha'penny if he could avoid it! Yet he'd always put a coin in the poor box at church, without fail. He had a good heart, he did.'

It was lovely to reminisce. There were so many stories gathered over the years, and it felt like a salve for our wounds to share them now. 'Then there was that time that he carried the fireguard, it must've been six foot wide, on the pram and walked it six miles to your place in Old Swan,' Nellie added, bursting into peals of laughter.

'Oh, I'd forgotten that! Yes, apparently he stopped the traffic, but he was determined to get that guard to me to protect me babbies.' Tears threatened to well up again. 'I don't think that fireguard was ever without a row of drying nappies on it after that.

'D'ye remember that funny story he used to tell us when he'd left the docks, that every night one of the dockers used to fill a wheelbarrow with sand and leave the site, the policeman would stop him and plunge his hand in the sand to search it, convinced he was thievin' somethin'.' I grinned as I recounted the tale.

Nellie cut in, 'And years later, when that policeman retired, he asked the docker at his leaving drink what he was nickin' and the docker told him it was the wheelbarrows! Didn't Da used to laugh at that one, eh?'

'He took your Tommy down to watch the Overhead Railway be dismantled in 1957. The "dockers' umbrella" they all used to call it as the track ran above the workers' heads, protectin' them from the rain. He loved those docklands . . .' I sighed.

'And when he swore, he never used the real bad words, he used his own version "James's Church" for "Jesus Christ",' said Nellie, holding my hand.

'And if he was really angry, he'd throw his cap on the floor and jump on it!' I joined in, the memories coming thick and fast.

'He was a gentleman through and through,' Nellie added. 'It's hard to believe he's now buried in the Catholic section at Allerton Cemetery, rather than here with us at home.'

At that we both stopped talking. There was nothing left to say. We had our stories, they were all we had left of the best father two girls could ever have. After losing our brother Tommy he'd never been the same. I would've given anything to relieve him of that loss. But he was far from pain now, and for that I was grateful at least.

I never forgot those words of his, though I denied them in myself for years to come. For so long, if I was honest, since I was a child, I'd felt trapped in my domestic sphere, even though I adored my siblings, then later my children, and stood by my marriage vows.

Then, one day in the mid-1970s, I don't recall the month or the year, I stood gazing out across the estate, the patterns of the leaves from the tree-lined avenue waving against my window pane, the sun bobbing in through my pulled curtains, I suddenly knew that I had the strength to leave Jo, to become my own person at long last.

Perhaps it was my father's death, his final words to me that taught me all those years ago that life was meant for living to the full, that sadness was a blessing to help me change things in my life that weren't right. Or perhaps it was the fact that my children had grown up, left home to forge their own paths. It may simply have been a moment when I finally, finally had enough of my married life with Jo and yearned to break free, to fly at my own pace, under the weight of my own wings at last.

I'd been a wife and a mother for more years than I cared to remember. Perhaps now it was my turn. I hadn't had the courage before. I lived by the rules of my faith and my society, yet the world was changing. Things were different these days, more relaxed, more forgiving of people's changing needs and situations. I needed to breathe again, and I knew in that moment that I wouldn't ever be able to until I left Jo.

The door to the kitchen opened behind me. Jo entered, rubbing his hands through his still-thick hair and scratching the stubble on his chin. He was still a well-built man, muscly, with a definite presence. Wherever you were, you knew if Jo Clarke was in the room. But today, his shadow didn't worry or alarm me, I held out his morning cup of strong tea and simply said, 'Jo, I'm getting a divorce.'

For a moment, all that could be heard was the sound of a bird calling from a nearby branch. Jo looked confused, just for a second, before guffawing in his loud voice, with laughter. 'Go 'ed, Maggie, you had me going there for a minute!'

He clearly had no idea that I wasn't making a joke. This was real, and I was absolutely in earnest. I waited calmly until he stopped, and before he could sit himself down at the table to eat, I said again, 'Jo, I'm not jokin', like, I'm leaving ye. I'm goin' into town today and I'm goin' to see me solicitor. It's over, Jo.'

His face looked blank, and then he erupted. He raised his voice at me for a while, and I waited until he'd finished, then smiled sadly and left the room to collect my things for my outing.

He followed behind me, sneering, saying he'd wanted to leave me 'a million times' but that he'd taken pity on me and stayed. I said nothing. I was weary to my bones, and I had absolutely nothing left to say to this man who I'd stuck by, and made excuses for, for too many years. It felt to me like there was a glass wall between me and Jo now. I could see him rage in disbelief but his words didn't pierce me, didn't touch me like they used to. I'd disconnected from him and from our marriage, and for me, all there was left to do was to end it as quickly and as efficiently as possible.

Those next few weeks were awkward to say the least. We each lived in the same house, using half of it each without verbalising the boundaries of our adjacent territory. I told the children one by one, hoping they'd understand, and to

my surprise there was little condemnation and much acceptance. I think some of them, perhaps Eileen and Joe, thought
I should have left sooner, but I like to think I left because it
was the right time for me.

The formalities went through without much of a fuss.
We had nothing really to divide up between us. I was just
glad to be rid of him and his ways. I stayed in the house,
and Jo would go to live with a friend until he got himself
sorted.

When the day came for him to leave, we both stood at the
doorway. Jo had a large suitcase stuffed with his nice clothes
and I didn't even begrudge him those any more. I took a last
look at him, and before he could speak I turned away, shutting the door as I did so. It was the look of sheer puzzlement
on Jo's face that I remember most clearly. He thought he was
a model husband perhaps? Or he thought that I was such an
obedient wife that I'd never do this to him? I don't know, I
never asked. He'd fed and clothed his children over the years.
We'd had some good times in the beginning when he'd been
in good humour, before the daily drudgery of rearing child
after child, but those times were fewer and fewer as the years
passed. He hadn't been all terrible, but that part of my life
was over, and it wasn't a moment too soon.

He won't ever put me down again, I said to myself, *he won't
ever belittle me in front of the children*, I added, liking the
sound of my thoughts.

'He won't ever criticise me, or spend our money, or waste
his time in the pub. He won't ever *EVER* hurt me like that
again.' This time I said it loudly, with emphasis, with satisfaction. The list of things I would never have to put up with
again grew longer and longer as the day wore on.

I didn't have to cook that evening either, as it was just me
curled up on the sofa, and so I made a couple of slices of toast

and a warm mug of Horlicks and I settled down to listen to the birdsong at the end of the day. It was a moment of pure unadulterated peace, without having to worry what state my husband would be in on his return from goodness knows where. I thought, *I have never experienced a better night than this*.

I knew that surviving by myself would be difficult, but I had friends locally who helped out, such was our way. My best friends on the estate, Biddy Dalton, Maggie Duncalfe and Nora Williams, all pitched in over those next few days. When they were younger, our children had run in and out of each other's homes. The joke had been that we kept lending each other the same ten-bob note, which circulated around our households as we lend it to each other to buy the food we needed each day. I can honestly say that I never had a lonely moment as the days and weeks passed.

When I confessed to my priest what I'd done, he gave me the expected penance but I could hear the compassion in his voice. I may have said, 'Bless me Father for I have sinned . . .' in the confessional box, but inside me my heart was singing a new, unfamiliar, quiet song of my own. I know that divorce is a sin within my church, but surely happiness couldn't be? And when the two came together it was more than I understood to know if I'd done wrong or not. Whatever my faith taught me, I knew that I had the blessing of my own father, Thomas Riley

I knew things wouldn't be easy without my husband. Yet my children had grown into bright, happy adults. I mused on them all: my Rita who loved the Beatles and was so caring; my Eileen, who was so laid-back, nothing ruffled her feathers; my Joe, who had the gift of the gab; my Denny, the witty one who played guitar; my peacemaker daughter Ann, who always looked fashionable; my Kathleen, who was the organised one; my Kevin the comedian; and my John, who was quiet and dignified. They were children I could be proud of, and they were now making their way in the world as adults, some of them with children of their own. I didn't have to worry about them. I didn't have to stay with Jo to keep a roof over their heads. They had flown the nest, and it was my time to spread my wings and soar. I knew there'd be times I'd need help, but I also knew that I had the support of my children, my friends and the church to see me through the tough bits, and to share the simple joys of a life lived in freedom.

CHAPTER 20

Leaving Liverpool

1981

'More than a hundred white and coloured youths fought a pitched battle against the police,' said the newsman from the telly. I sat watching my television screen aghast, not wanting to believe this was happening in my beloved Liverpool. 'Some were as young as twelve, the oldest no more than twenty. It lasted for eight hours and at the end of it Merseyside's chief constable said it was a planned attack. "We were set up," he said. The worst of the rioting came just after dawn, when police faced a hail of stones, bottles, iron bars and petrol bombs . . .'

The screen flickered, showing upturned cars on fire, lines of black-clothed policemen, wounded men crouched on pavements. It bore no resemblance to the city I knew, the community I had loved since a child. The Toxteth Riots broke out in Upper Parliament Street on a muggy, suffocating July day in 1981. I sat at home, the TV on, watching in disbelief, understanding the frustrations of a generation of young people without work and prospects, yet feeling a sense of shock that people could be so wicked to each other on both sides of the argument. My faith taught me to love thy neighbour, and me of all people knew what it was to grow up in grinding poverty, but the thought of staging a riot chilled me to the core. It brought back memories of the Orange march, the hatred shown by usually peace-loving friends and neighbours who turned into excrement-hurling strangers. There had always been a sense of deep division within my part of the city; Catholics against Proddys. It was the way it was, and I supposed that nothing had changed, but to me it now looked like the poor versus the rich. I didn't like this angry feel again, in the streets that had for so long been home to me and mine. I was too old for conflict. I wanted peace and certainty, and looking at those images, that sense of rage imbedded within such young people, I felt suddenly sad.

The phone rang at that moment. I got up to pick up the receiver and it was Eileen.

'Y'all right, Mam?' she asked, and I replied, my usual, 'Yes luv, I'm all right, don't ye go worryin' about me.'

'Have ye seen the news, Mam?' came her swift reply.

For months now, Eileen had been urging me to move down to London to be near her, Ann and Rita. This upsurge of violence had got me wondering if it wasn't time to go.

'Yes, I've got me telly on our Eileen. Don't know what's got into people, we'd never have rioted in my day,' I replied, squinting over at the screen to watch the footage shot by those brave cameramen.

At the other end, Eileen sighed. 'Things are different now, Mam, which is why I want ye to come down here and live near us. I can't pop up there, now can I, and see if yer all right, but I can if yer in London. Look, think about it, eh? I'll call ye tomorrow.'

'All right luv, you take care of yerself,' I replied. The phone clicked and then buzzed as the call ended, and went back to my lounge.

I hadn't wanted to admit to myself that I no longer recognised my city as a place of community and family. It seemed like an alien land these days to me. I was sixty-one years old, and I wasn't getting any younger. Perhaps it was time for me to make the move? So many of my friends from the old days had moved away, though Nellie was still in Liverpool.

I barely knew my neighbours except to say hello and smile. We didn't pop in and out of each other's houses any more for a cup of loose tea leaves or a slice or two of bread to tide us over. We didn't gossip while we hung out the washing or look after each other's children while their mothers went to work in the city. No, things were different now. Perhaps Eileen was right, times had moved on and I had to move with them?

I mused on this as I made a cup of tea and sat watching till the end of the news. Afterwards I switched it off and sat, sipping the hot liquid, and wondered if I could ever happily leave the place I was born. I had so many memories bound up in the roads that sprawled the docklands and Scottie Road. I hadn't lived in that area for a good few years now, and I hadn't been back to visit for ages. Yet those streets still had a deep pull for me, a memory of lost times, lost people, and I wasn't sure I could abandon it completely, it would be like cutting out a part of myself.

I thought back to the childhood I had before our mam left and my life as a surrogate mother began, laughing and playing in the filthy cobbled courts, dodging in and out of those hellish places, weaving between billowing washing, clattering children, catcalling women and the horse and carts. There were gas lighters, and dockers, coalmen and veg hawkers with their hand-drawn carts, like my mam Mary's. There was noise and bustle from dawn till midnight, against the backdrop of the smoke and stench from the factories that lined the salt-encrusted docks, the ships' masts swaying with the deep currents of that treacherous stretch of the Mersey, the rumble of the overland railway that snaked along the lengths of the numerous docks.

It was a place of adventure, of chaos and desperate living conditions. TB was rife. We crawled with lice, scratching at our clothes and our skin all day, so much so that we hardly noticed. Bugs scattered across the walls, rats darted between the open drains, as boys crossing their legs banged on the doors of the foul outdoor lavvies at the entrance to the courts that the families all shared. The smell of the dirt, the disease, the human and animal excrement, the spices from the warehouses and the sharp sting of the tobacco factory filled the air, making a heady cocktail that was given relief only by the Atlantic streams that blew across the river, leaving us shivering in its wake but glad to gulp down cleaner air.

How could I leave those turgid waters that churned at the edge of our watery home? How could I turn my back on the place that our Tommy, my eighteen-year-old brother, left and never returned to? It felt like I would be leaving him behind forever. The courts were long gone, of course. Yet, between the bombs and the demolition, something more vital than dirt and disease was lost, in my mind. Our community had dissolved over the years. Our tight-knit world had slowly unravelled as people were rehomed into those bright new council homes, separating families who'd lived in each other's pockets for generations, while others' moved for work or for family reasons. That's how it was. Time couldn't move backwards. The relentless march forward of history would only go one way, and now it felt like it was my turn to look towards the future.

When Eileen rang the next day, she asked me if I'd thought any more about leaving Liverpool. I paused, then I said I had, and I would go to London. I don't think Eileen thought I'd ever do it, and she sounded so pleased that I realised by going there I'd at least be able to stop her worrying about me.

My daughters also had children, my grandchildren, and of course I missed seeing them grow up. The decision was easy to make, but heart wrenching to follow through. I knew it was the right thing to do, but I also knew that I would forever look wistfully at the Thames and wish it was a different river, one with sandbanks and changing tides, one that looked to the west for inspiration, rather than inwards upon itself.

It didn't take long to pack up and relocate. Taking the train from Liverpool Lime Street Station, I glanced across the sea of people moving, all busy, all rushing through life. Perhaps, I thought to myself, they had the right idea. Perhaps it wasn't wise to linger in the corridors, the winding passageways of the past. Perhaps, now, it was better to lift my face to the sunlight and look away at last, away from the echoes of my memories, the imprints of the people I had loved and lost, and look forward at last. My soul was forever in Liverpool but life had other plans for me, and so I did what any sensible woman would do. I said a fond farewell to the past and turned my heart to what would come, and all the joys life might bring me. As a final gesture I blew my city a discreet kiss, loaded my suitcase onto the train and turned away. When the train moved out of the station, I didn't look back.

Eileen had put me down for a small, neat one-bedroom council flat in south London, near to where she was living. It took me a long time to settle, though.

Every day I missed hearing the Scouse accent. 'Y'all right, queen?' or 'I'm made up for ye.' The London accent seemed harsher, whereas I thought the Liverpool lilt more caring, more human in its way. Those streets, those people, those sayings, smells and noises of Liverpool still ran through my veins like blood, but they became memories rather than lived experience, and I had to allow that to be enough.

Many times I'd make myself a jam butty just for the memory of them. I remembered scraping the brightly coloured red jam on a slice of white or brown bread, depending on whether there was rationing or not, and watching my siblings first, then later my own children, line up at the counter to receive their simple lunch as the drying nappies dripped over their heads and the weak sunlight filtered past the grimy windows into our rundown flats. I would laugh as I thought of those days. How little we had! And yet, how excited the children would be to get a jam butty in the middle of the day! Those youngsters on the telly really had no idea of that kind of hardship, but each generation has troubles of its own, I knew that, and couldn't blame them for their obvious frustration.

If I was feeling really homesick, I'd get a pan of scouse on the cooker and invite over my daughters to eat it with me. As we all sat round in my small, sunny flat, I'd reminisce about the days when my father would come in from his shift, kiss us all before going to the outside water pump to splash his soot and sweat-streaked face. I remember the welcome sound of his docker's boots clomping back into the flat in Athol Street. He'd fling his cap and coat on a nearby chair and draw himself close to the range, whatever the weather outside, to warm his bones.

Never one to shirk his duties, he'd always come in with a few extra veggies or even a beef bone or scraps of lamb to add to the pot. I'd chop the onions, add the barley and gravy, then there'd be neeps or spuds with a few herbs if we had them, and some chopped carrots, and the whole thing would simmer down into thick, nourishing scouse for us all to share. The conversation around the dinner table would hush as I ladled out the stew, Tommy and Nellie holding out their plates, their faces concentrating on not spilling a precious drop. I'd cut the bread, spread it with butter if we had it, always giving the largest portion to my da, before finally doling out some for myself. We'd pray together, holding each meal sacred, then eat.

The chatter would begin again. Tommy would recount his stories of daring deeds, collecting fallen coal from the gasworks' carts, or playing marbles in the alleys, while Nellie would sing or hum to herself. Da would sit quietly eating, enjoying his children, looking at us with such pride that I would always feel the warmth of those days, however chilled I became through my marriage to Jo.

Those days were over, the good and the bad. They were consigned to my family's history, but they were good days, they were days when we had each other, and that counted for everything.

Afterword

Maggie created a family that has become nothing less than a dynasty in its own right. To date, she has twenty grandchildren, twenty-two great-grandchildren and four great-great-grandchildren. While her eldest daughter Rita sadly passed away in 2014, survived by her daughter Marina and son Peter, the rest of her children are thriving, living productive lives.

At the time of writing Maggie is ninety-six years old. The first time I spoke to her daughter Eileen, in 2015, Maggie was cooking her daughter sausage and chips in the background, proving that for some age really is merely a number. When her granddaughter Marina married, Maggie gave her a frying pan, saying she could 'either cook chips with it or hit her husband over the head with it', showing her keen scouse humour is still going strong.

Acknowledgements

My thanks go to all of Maggie's family for their support and encouragement while researching Maggie's life, but in particular to Eileen Montaut, Kevin Clarke, Tommy Horrocks and Marina Dunn.

The staff – and members of the public – at the Liverpool Central Library Archive and Record Office were all unfailing in their attempts to help me gather dates and data, and I am extremely grateful to them all.

A huge thank you to Publisher Anna Valentine, Emma Smith and all the team at Orion Publishing, and my agent Jane Graham Maw of Graham Maw Christie Literary Agents, for their vision and belief that Maggie's story deserves telling, reminding us all that the resilience and fortitude, the joys and loves of women during wartime and beyond are an essential part of our emotional heritage.

It has been a privilege to share a small part of such a great lady's journey through life, and to be inspired by her strength and down-to-earth wisdom. Thank you, Maggie Clarke.

Cathryn Kemp